LEADERSHIP EXCELLENCE COURSE

BUILDING A DURABLE LEGACY OF QUALITY

Participant Name

DAVID BENSON

**David Benson, MBA
Leadership Coach**

Leadership is the purposeful advancement of a group vision. Excellent leadership develops people.

—David Benson

Published by David Benson Coaching
North Logan, Utah. See www.DavidBenson.us for full contact information.

Copyright © 2018-2019 by David Benson

All rights reserved. Neither this book nor any part thereof may be used, reproduced, transmitted, distributed, or stored in any manner or format whatever without prior written permission of the author, except in the case of brief quotations embodied in critical articles or reviews. Book and cover design by David Benson.

Liability and Warranty Disclaimer. While every effort has been made to ensure informational accuracy in this book, the author and publisher do not assume and hereby disclaim any liability for loss, damage, or disruption caused by omissions, errors, or content use of any type whatsoever. No explicit nor implied warranty or guarantee is extended. Narrative elements in this work spawn from the author's experience, study, and imagination and are used in a fictitious manner.

Printed in the United States of America
Second Edition | March 08, 2019 (version 2019.03.5) | First Published 01/15/2018
10 9 8 7 6 5 4 3 2

LCCN: 2019902777
ISBN-13: 978-1-7337711-3-9 (paperback)
BISAC Subject Headings: in BUSINESS & ECONOMICS
    BUS071000 … / Leadership, BUS066000 … / Training,
    BUS059000 … / Skills, BUS041000 … / Management;
    SEL040000 SELF-HELP / Communication & Social Skills

If you purchased this book without a cover, be aware that this book is stolen property. It was reported as "unsold and destroyed" to the publisher, and neither the author nor the publisher has received any payment for this "stripped" book.

Please visit www.DavidBenson.us for background and offering information.

Contents at a Glance

Warm Welcome 0.2
    Leadership Excellence Model (LEM) 0.2
    What to Expect 0.3
    Excellent Leadership 0.4
Total Engagement Track 1.1
    Confident Engagement 2.1
    Inspired Engagement 3.1
    Endorsed Engagement 4.1
    Empowered Engagement 5.1
    Enthusiastic Engagement 6.1
    Cultivated Engagement 7.1
Dynamic Presentations Track 8.1
    Genuine Presentations 9.1
    Stirring Presentations 10.1
    Precise Presentations 11.1
    Discerning Presentations 12.1
    Persuasive Presentations 13.1
    Guided Presentations 14.1
Effective Management Track 15.1
    Candid Management 16.1
    Resolute Management 17.1
    Refined Management 18.1
    Vigorous Management 19.1
    Cooperative Management 20.1
    Mentored Management 21.1
Training Culmination 22.1
    Congratulations 22.2
    Most Significant Benefit 22.3
    Training Evaluation 22.4
    Transformation Project 22.5
    References 22.7
    About the Coach 22.11

LEADERSHIP

WARM WELCOME

Congratulations on deciding to participate in this professional training! Your sincere desire to sharpen skills and improve performance is truly praiseworthy. We confidently expect to see stunning, positive results as we apply the concepts and embrace the coaching that will guide growth.

Our time is valuable. Please be prepared to fully contribute, focusing on our activities together for the most advantage. Our training laboratory is a respectful, productive venue to practice principles and to build character.

Leadership Excellence Model (LEM)

Constructing an exceptional edifice to last a lifetime takes deliberate effort, carefully placing each brick and beam until the structure is complete. So it is with developing great leadership: experiences build on each other until we become our desired leader, benefitting our professional pursuits, our formal organizations, and the people in our personal spheres of influence.

Leadership Excellence	Total Engagement	Dynamic Presentations	Effective Management
Intrepid Integrity	Confident	Genuine	Candid
Real Motivation	Inspired	Stirring	Resolute
Sound Strategy	Endorsed	Precise	Refined
Pivotal Quality	Empowered	Discerning	Vigorous
Heroic Altruism	Enthusiastic	Persuasive	Cooperative
Crucial Coaching	Cultivated	Guided	Mentored

Distinct workshops are designed to develop core skills. When combined, they act as building blocks for creating higher-level talents and refining habits. Series focus on the six essential leadership characteristics, in rows, while Tracks concentrate on three crucial leadership themes, in columns. The Leadership Excellence Course addresses all 18 workshops.

Coaching

Count on practical, constructive coaching to ensure effective application of the techniques we practice. Rely on useful feedback in the moment—whether individually, with peers, or in small and larger groups—designed to stretch abilities and provide challenging insights. Our coaching is founded on esteem and kindness.

What to Expect

Professional development training represents a significant investment. We want to make the most of our experience through thoughtful discussion, group activities, careful practice, immediate feedback, and assignments to provide extra value. An eager, positive attitude will result in a fantastic experience for ourselves and others.

Anticipate arriving early to each event so that we can start on time. We will also end on time—at the latest—though the coach often will be available for limited post-event conversations. Skills development is integrated and progressive, so please participate in every activity. Appropriate business attire is recommended, and limiting electronic device usage is endorsed.

This participant workbook is yours to keep. Make liberal notes to augment learning, and refer to it frequently during and after the training. Pages for information, self-assessment, goals, analysis, reflection, application ideas, and future commitments will help guide the experience.

Everyone will be encouraged to commit to future assignments to polish covered topics, and to prepare for upcoming ones. Completing each task will result in the most improvement, and participants should feel free to pair with others at the event to foster accountability.

In the End

Leadership development can be a very personal venture, and though we are ultimately responsible for our own growth, we can benefit from and contribute to the progress of fellow participants. As others report on their experiences, record your reactions for future reference. We will have occasions to acknowledge their evolution, and recognize their influence on our own progress.

As we see the significant benefits from this training, consider exposing others to the same experience so they might also profit.

In some cases, an optional Master Project may be available for participants desiring to apply the training topics to a specific situation within their organization. Please direct inquires to the coach.

LEADERSHIP

Excellent Leadership

Leadership is the purposeful advancement of a group vision. Excellent leadership develops people. It should be a part of everything we do in business, community, and personal interactions. Leaders start with integrity about who they are, striving for honesty in all interactions. Their motivation springs from an understanding of why they do what they do, driven to create a better world. They form a clear strategic plan, a path for achieving success in forms they have determined for themselves. They strive for quality along the way, treating others with altruism and being willing to coach those also wishing to succeed. Leaders demonstrate, illuminate, activate, dedicate, appreciate, and circulate.

This vibrant, inspiring course is based on the LEM, and energizes participants to improve their performance as leaders. It is divided into three integrated, progressive tracks or themes designed to add value: Total Engagement, Dynamic Presentations, and Effective Management. We express our influence as leaders as we engage employees, present publically, and manage teams. Across tracks are six series devoted to key leadership characteristics: Integrity, Motivation, Strategy, Quality, Altruism, and Coaching.

Sincere Admonition

The leadership characteristics and principles we are about to experience together are true and faithful. They have made a significant difference for good in many lives. As we faithfully embrace, practice, and then share them with those we respect, we will appreciate the same mighty changes. The leadership world is ours to possess. Let us be excellent!

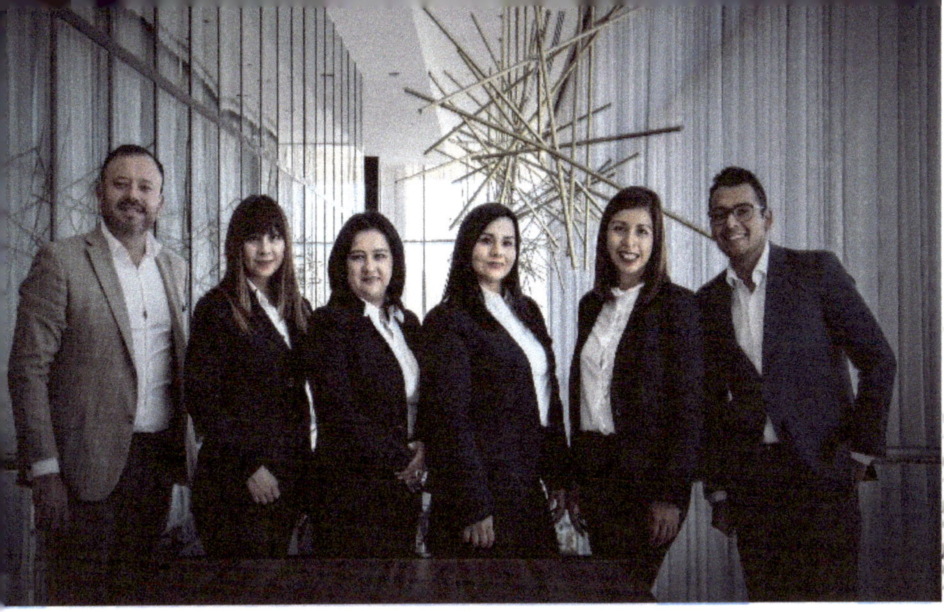

TOTAL ENGAGEMENT TRACK
Uniting Efforts for Maximum Success

Participant Name

ENGAGEMENT

Leadership and Engagement

We have heard that the only constant in the universe is change, and the professional development world is no different. It seems new research is regularly leading to new models, techniques, and fads. Learners pursuing leadership excellence need only focus on enduring principles to succeed, aiming at clear, written, vibrant targets to measure progress.

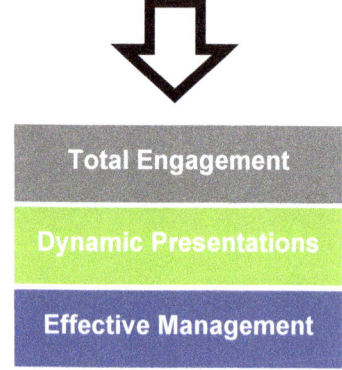

Total Engagement Track

Engagement is the personal drive for organizational excellence. It is achieved as people feel increasingly valued and connected. Progression along the value continuum starts with confidence, then inspiration, endorsement, empowerment, enthusiasm, and finally cultivation. As part of the Leadership Excellence course, this Total Engagement Track will pursue how to apply the six leadership characteristics to ourselves and those with whom we interact.

A person's perceived sense of value peaks as they experience enthusiasm and are cultivated by a caring supervisor. It is only then that they are able to approach full engagement. People must be fully engaged in their organization or cause in order to effectively lead. The sense of engagement can only be as strong as the organization's commitment to the individual, or the "organizational drive for personal excellence." In short, help those in your circles of influence feel important, cared for, and valuable.

  ENGAGEMENT

Introducing Engagement

The word engagement conjures a variety of images, from a simple dinner appointment to a formal betrothal, and yet the situations all have similar aspects in common. There is a sense of commitment as to time, place, or activity. A decision has been made and now it is time to get in gear and interact as promised. There are at least two parties involved, and sometimes not in a friendly way, as in engaging with the enemy. Beyond the physical presence, there is a sense of emotional or intellectual commitment, as in a responsibility to perform on a job or contract, either as the worker as the proprietor.

As Bob Kelleher explained in his book, *Louder than Words*:

> *For engagement to exist there must be mutual commitment between the employer and the employee, wherein the employer is helping the employee reach his or her untapped potential and the employee is helping the employer meet and surpass its business goals.*

Original Quote

The original definition of engagement is geared toward the relationship between employer and employee, the organization and its members. Most characterizations, including that of Bob Kelleher above, take this stance. But even in the initial explanation is room for a broader application. We engage in a large number of relationships and situations, our professional circumstances being just one possibility.

> *… the harnessing of organisation members' selves to their work roles; in engagement, people employ and express themselves physically, cognitively, and emotionally during role performances.*
>
> —William Khan, 1990

ENGAGEMENT   David Benson Coaching

Engagement Self-Assessment

Please frankly assess yourself for each leadership skill below based on your current situation using a scale from 0-10 (*never* to *always*). Rate your abilities before training, then again after the training is complete.

Leadership Skills to Measure	Before	After	+ / -
1. I understand engagement and its impact.			
2. I am self-confident in difficult situations.			
3. My shared values better my relationships.			
4. My energy matches the message to communicate.			
5. I encourage others to share their opinions.			
6. My personal ambitions align with group goals.			
7. I encourage autonomy in my staff.			
8. Teams deliberately celebrate achieved milestones.			
9. Listening is an active, focused activity for me.			
10. I regularly show appreciation for employee efforts.			
11. Performance reviews are heartening and hopeful.			
12. Coaching personnel is a regular part of my day.			
Assessment Totals (120 points max.)			

Once the engagement training has ended and the above assessment complete, please identify the most significant value, benefit, or gain for:

13. You as an individual, professionally, personally, or otherwise.

_____

_____

14. Your organization, business, community, or other relationships.

_____

_____

Personality Change

The phrase *you are what you eat* may be true to some degree, but the more important realization is that we are what we experience. We are what we think, feel, express, and do. Our personality is the intricate blend of our emotional and behavioral characteristics or traits that uniquely distinguish us from each other. We form our personality by our thoughts and actions.

Improvement only occurs when we make a decision to shift our emotions and behavior in some direction. Changing either without the other is insufficient, and though excellence can be difficult, it can be achieved when we work towards it.

$$PC = EC \times IC \times BC$$

Transforming Engagement

Think of the many possible benefits you might realize through this total engagement training. What do you want to improve about yourself as an individual or a leader? How about in your teams, or in your work situation generally? What admirable qualities, habits, or processes do you see elsewhere that you would like to adopt for yourself? What would you need to get out of this training to make it completely and utterly worthwhile?

_____

_____

_____

_____

_____

_____

_____

_____

ENGAGEMENT

Becoming Engaged

Much research has been performed regarding employee engagement, how to define it, current trends, why it is important, and how to grow it. These inquiries often lead to new models, techniques, and fads. Learners pursuing total engagement need only focus on enduring principles to succeed, aiming at clear, written, vibrant targets to measure progress.

Identity
We wear many hats in many divergent situations. For the purposes of this training, determine your primary title, position, or role in your organization.

I	Please record **who** you are for our training purposes.

Vision
An inspiring statement of purpose or motivation describes our future, ideal situation. Briefly state your vision of a more engaged leader.

●	Please record **why** you want to increase team engagement.

Mission
A single, ambitious, overarching goal defines what we will do to realize our vision. This has more detail, covering all aspects of our work. Subordinate milestones and tasks support it. Briefly state your engagement mission.

↱	Please record **what** you will do to achieve your engagement vision.

CONFIDENT ENGAGEMENT
Building Integrity to Grow Value

So glad to be here. So pleased to meet friends old and new ...

CONFIDENT

David Benson Coaching

Becoming Confident

We start our journey at the beginning, creating a foundation solid enough to support our lofty leadership aspirations. Confidence is said to be an assurance, state of belief, or firm trust in someone or something. It can be an attitude of certitude, a driving faith pushing us to achieve.

Personal Insight: Confident

What does being confident mean to you? How does it relate to our opening activity/discussion? In what ways will becoming more confident improve your current situation?

_____

_____

_____

Integrity and Confident

Being confident in ourselves is the beginning of integrity, the first key characteristic of leadership. More than mere honesty, integrity encompasses being true to who we are, and to the idealistic self we hope to become. It is about being honorable, reliable, trustworthy, and constant.

Engagement and Confident

When people feel confident, they have started the path to engagement. They have a sense in their own worth, the significance of their skills, and the depth of their potential to positively influence their organizations. Confident employees are ready to contribute to the success of their companies. They are typically comfortable with the requirements of their positions, and at ease in ordinary and expected work situations.

Value Continuum for Total Engagement						
Disengaged →		Partially Engaged		→		Fully Engaged
Unvalued	Confident	Inspired	Endorsed	Empowered	Enthusiastic	Cultivated

INTREPID INTEGRITY > TOTAL ENGAGEMENT > LEADERSHIP EXCELLENCE

CONFIDENT

Training Objectives

Workshop objectives represent small goals designed to help us develop the leadership characteristic being deliberated. They provide both clear direction for our training activities, and a method for measuring successful application of the related content. They connect to the leadership skills we evaluated as part of our self-assessment at the start of our training.

As we diligently embrace these objectives, we will perceive positive changes in our performance and personality.

Confident Training Objectives	♥
1. Understand the importance of engagement and to start the path to full engagement	
2. Practice confidence in uncomfortable circumstances to produce trust in ourselves	
3. Increase self-confidence in especially difficult situations to face them with poise	

Linking to Engagement

Think back to the vision and mission for increasing total engagement that we considered at the beginning of the training. Reflect on how this characteristic relates to our desire to become more engaged.

=	How does becoming more confident support those aims? Why is increasing confidence critical to becoming a successful leader?

> *No one can make you feel inferior without your consent.*
> —Eleanor Roosevelt

CONFIDENT

Understanding Engagement

There are dozens, perhaps hundreds of definitions for engagement. Which one best matches the aspects that are important to you?

Original…

> … the harnessing of organisation members' selves to their work roles; in engagement, people employ and express themselves physically, cognitively, and emotionally during role performances.
> —William Khan, 1990

More Modern…

> … the extent to which employees feel passionate about their jobs, are committed to the organization, and put discretionary effort into their work.
> —Deloitte University Press, 2017

Most Succinct…

> The personal drive for organizational excellence.
> —David Benson, 2017

- ➢ Personal = internal, emotional, me, my whole person
- ➢ Drive = dedication, passion, motivation, inspiring
- ➢ Organizational = bigger cause, unselfish, long duration
- ➢ Excellence = superior, beyond the minimum

Engagement Levels

Engagement is typically measured in three different levels, with varying degrees of engagement for each. The 2016 United States levels are shown below. Where do you fall on the spectrum? Members of your team?

- ➢ Fully engaged………………33%
- ➢ Partially engaged……………51%
- ➢ Actively disengaged…………16%

INTREPID INTEGRITY > TOTAL ENGAGEMENT > LEADERSHIP EXCELLENCE

CONFIDENT

Measuring Our Engagement

Consider your situation back at your organization. Do you feel fully engaged, or a little less? Maybe not at all? What would you estimate is the level of engagement for your team members? Measure yourself and your team on the following scale: A = 2 points, B = 1 point, C = 0 points.

I	Score each question in both columns	Me	Team
❖	**Why are you here?**		
a.	Looking for insights on how to improve our current situation.		
b.	The boss asked me to come. I thought it might be fun.		
c.	Anything to get away for a bit!		
❖	**What are you missing?**		
a.	Fulfilling work on an exciting project; this better be good!		
b.	Same ole, same ole.		
c.	Who cares?		
❖	**How do you perceive others are behaving?**		
a.	They know what needs to be done, and I am sure they are doing it.		
b.	Hopefully following their instructions. They will call if they need help.		
c.	Probably goofing off.		
Totals (0-1 = dis-, 2-4 = partially, 5-6 = fully)			

_____

_____

INTREPID INTEGRITY > TOTAL ENGAGEMENT > LEADERSHIP EXCELLENCE

CONFIDENT

Practicing Confidence

Leadership starts with who we are. Before we can appreciate what motivates us, we need to know who we are. The influence of our family, friends, colleagues, supervisors, and mentors have large roles to play in this understanding. Perhaps above all else, the sum of our experiences, the highs and lows as we interact with people we esteem and who challenge us, influences who we become personally and professionally.

People are sometimes hesitant in new or uncomfortable situations, but the engaged employee is ever more courageous in those cases. We can practice techniques to increase our confidence and build reserves when such occasions present themselves.

Greet with Confidence

Here are some simple ways we can demonstrate a confident manner.

- ➢ Prepare our message
- ➢ Positive, upbeat tone of voice
- ➢ Open, friendly body language

Voice Inflection

We sometimes rush through our own name when we greet others, making it difficult for our audience to understand us, and planting seeds of doubt in their minds about our self-confidence. Inflecting our voice upwards (higher pitch) when pronouncing our first name, pausing for a moment, then inflecting our voice downward (lower pitch) for our last name, creates a more clear and assured introduction.

❖ **Hello! My name is …**

David ǁ Benson

INTREPID INTEGRITY ➢ TOTAL ENGAGEMENT ➢ LEADERSHIP EXCELLENCE

Display Confidence

Formal introductions in front of a group are not unusual or new, but they continue to be uncomfortable for many people. It *is* public speaking after all, and can be quite nerve-racking! Now that we have practiced the voice inflection technique, let us use it to introduce ourselves in front of the room. Create a short introductory message with your full name, organization, position, why you are training with us, and one fact about yourself nobody else in the room would know. Be prepared for questions from the coach.

As other people introduce themselves, use the next page to remember names, organizations, and how they were able to perform well. How did they encourage us, use the techniques, and make confident connections?

Introduction Guidelines
Include all elements of our discussion in our introductions.

- Deliver the five points of our message:
    - Full name with voice inflection
    - Organization
    - Position
    - Why training with us?
    - Uncover a fun trivia
- Tone of voice
- Body language
- Respond to questions from the coach

> *Each time we face our fear, we gain strength, courage, and confidence in the doing.*
> —Theodore Roosevelt

INTREPID INTEGRITY ➢ TOTAL ENGAGEMENT > LEADERSHIP EXCELLENCE

CONFIDENT

Self-Confidence in Difficult Situations

In ordinary, typical circumstances we are often able to maintain our confidence. We are accustomed to the regular courses of events, know what to expect of them, and have had plenty of preparation and practice to deal with them. They are not very memorable. In fact, a greater risk than losing our poise is becoming complacent with the mundane.

It is in challenging situations that our confidence might be tested the most. Fortunately, we do get some experience with those situations, too, and they are almost always easy to remember. Recalling those instances and recognizing our strengths through them can be great sources of self-assurance to deal with current stressful or trying situations.

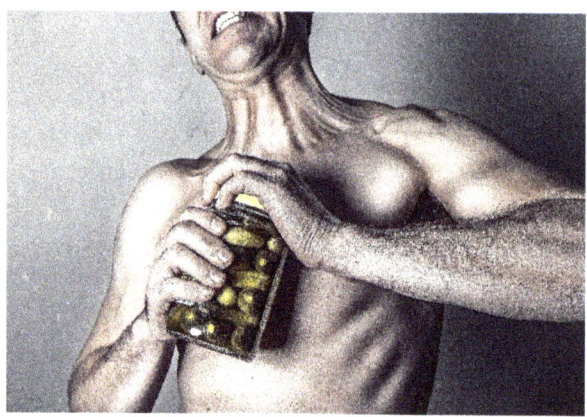

Some Examples

Examples of these experiences could include job interviews, work projects, testy customers, demanding supervisors, corporate buy-outs, graduations, promotions, personal successes and tragedies, and the like.

> ■ **Record examples of memorable experiences that made an impact.**

CONFIDENT

Memorable Moments (M&Ms)

We call these past experiences, which help shape and define who we are, Memorable Moments. They are especially memorable, some might say unforgettable, as they help us gain insights into our personality. We better understand what drives us, what is important to us, or what characteristics we embody.

Now that we have had a chance to consider some of our Memorable Moments, let us choose one that fills us with self-assurance.

- Pick a specific, past experience
- Briefly relate it in vivid detail, as if reliving it
- Recognize how I overcame an obstacle, failed a challenge, showed my true self
- Convey what this says about me, my traits
- Apply inspiration, courage, confidence from past experiences to current trials

I	What is your Memorable Moment? Add details to make it come alive. What does this experience say about me?

> *Giving people self-confidence is by far the most important thing I can do. Because then they will act.*
> —Jack Welch

INTREPID INTEGRITY > TOTAL ENGAGEMENT > LEADERSHIP EXCELLENCE

CONFIDENT   David Benson Coaching

Commitment: Memorable Moment

The quest for positive, exciting behavior change requires effort and stamina. It is for the strong-willed. In our workshop laboratory, we have explored activities contributing toward improved leadership. Continued practice and coaching will lead to mastery of the concepts and methods, ensuring solid, long-term results. Thank you for the authentic effort!

Prepare, Practice, and Report

Please prepare a Memorable Moment to practice outside of training and then report back to the lab participants. Consider your own development or the benefit of a co-worker when deciding who to involve.

I	**Prepare details for your Memorable Moment commitment.**

Memorable Moment Title:

Who to Involve:

Detailed Experience:

How I Overcame:

Why This Is Important:

INTREPID INTEGRITY > TOTAL ENGAGEMENT > LEADERSHIP EXCELLENCE

CONFIDENT

Commitment Report Observations

As participants relate their commitment experiences, carefully watch their delivery. Note how they applied the principles we have discussed. Did they cover all aspects of the commitment? What specifically did they do well? Where were opportunities to coach for even more progress? What did you observe that you would like to appreciate, recognize, or adopt for yourself?

Observation Notes: Name, Compliment, Proof
1.
2.
3.
4.

Commitment Report Personal Debrief

Review the commitment report you just delivered. Consider your own input and feedback from the coach and fellow participants. List everything you did well, circling the one success that was most meaningful to you. Identify one challenge that will add the most leadership value to when improved.

All My Successes

_____

_____

_____

My One Greatest Challenge

_____

CONFIDENT

Realized Benefits

We train to realize our vision, to develop tools to reach our goals, to become more excellent, and to assist others in doing the same. Having performed the related objectives, consider how they have moved us closer to attaining our vision and mission.

- [✓] Excellent
- [ ] Very good
- [ ] Good
- [ ] Average
- [ ] Poor

My Most Significant Benefit

Of all the benefits you may have experienced in this workshop, which one is the most significant for you, either professionally or personally? Why is this benefit essential to your leadership success?

_____

_____

_____

Benefitting Others

Our development serves to help those around us, our partners, teams, departments, and organizations. How will my most significant benefit impact those around me? Who in my circles of influence might also take advantage of this training to realize increased leadership success?

_____

_____

_____

_____

Helping Others Succeed

When we have a personal or professional breakthrough, we instinctively look to share the benefit with those close to us. We want them to succeed as well. Think of team members, colleagues, industry friends, even local neighbors who are seeking to improve their current situation, to become more excellent leaders. Who among them would be responsive to leadership training? Please speak with the coach about how to involve them in this very same or subsequent training events.

CONFIDENT

Confident Summary

Confidence in who we are and who we are becoming is central to maturing integrity, the first key characteristic of leadership. Confidence also forms the foundation for engaging ourselves and co-workers. As we understand engagement and its importance, we desire to move ourselves and others towards the fully engaged level. We can do this by perfecting activities such as displaying confidence and sharing memorable moments. We discussed three objectives:

1. Understand importance of engagement
2. Practice confidence when uncomfortable
3. Increase self-confidence in tough situations

There are a number of questions to contemplate as we summarize this workshop. Which concepts will result in the most positive impact if applied regularly? Which ones should you put into action right away? Why are those key? Which principles will make the most difference for improved leadership in your work situation? How can I most benefit the team that I am responsible for leading? In which area do I need to improve the most?

What additional activities can help improve on these skills?

How will my relationships progress as I apply these concepts?

CONFIDENT

Confident Conclusion

If you think you can do a thing, or think you can't do a thing, you're right.

—Henry Ford

Additional Notes

INSPIRED ENGAGEMENT
Finding Determination for the Effort

I have a dream. I move like I have a purpose ...

INSPIRED

Becoming Inspired

Certain beliefs, concepts, expectations, and desires are strong enough to move us to action. They inspire us to develop new skills, make hard changes, and become better people. Motivation is very personal, taking on a variety of forms and degrees of intensity.

Personal Insight: Inspired

What does being inspired mean to you? How does it relate to your current condition? In what ways will becoming more inspired improve your situation?

_____

_____

_____

Motivation and Inspired

Being inspired leads us to motivation, the second key characteristic of leadership. A driving force, motivation is what pushes us to become the leaders we wish to be. It involves understanding our values, why things are important to us, and forming a vision for the future.

Engagement and Inspired

When people are inspired, they start to move beyond their individual desires and contribute to larger causes. They take pride in their groups, agree with their purpose and vision, and want to see them succeed. Inspired employees share many of the same values with their companies and co-workers, and receive respect for unique ideals. They believe that their organizations are worthwhile places to devote their energies.

Value Continuum for Total Engagement							
Disengaged →			Partially Engaged →			Fully Engaged	
Unvalued	Confident	Inspired	Endorsed	Empowered	Enthusiastic	Cultivated	

Training Objectives

Workshop objectives represent small goals designed to help us develop the leadership characteristic being deliberated. They provide both clear direction for our training activities, and a method for measuring successful application of the related content. They connect to the leadership skills we evaluated as part of our self-assessment at the start of our training.

As we diligently embrace these objectives, we will perceive positive changes in our performance and personality.

Inspired Training Objectives	♥
1. Identify key benefits of full engagement to develop inspired group members	
2. Explore values shared within organizations to establish closer relationships	
3. Animate communications within teams to make our desires more convincing	

Linking to Engagement

Think back to the vision and mission for increasing total engagement that we considered at the beginning of the training. Reflect on how this characteristic relates to our desire to become more engaged.

=	How does becoming more inspired support those aims? Why is increasing inspiration critical to becoming a successful leader?

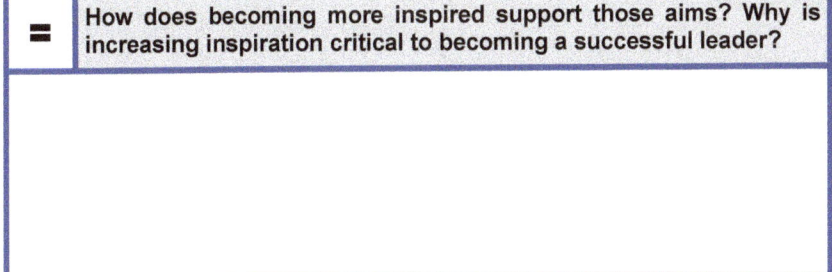

Our chief want is someone who will inspire us to be what we know we could be.
—Ralph Waldo Emerson

INSPIRED   David Benson Coaching

Full Engagement Key Benefits

What does it matter to us if we or our teams are fully engaged? There are plenty of reasons! Which one is most motivating to you? When compared to other businesses, fully-engaged companies are doing very well.

#	Benefit	%
1.	Higher customer satisfaction by…	10%
2.	Higher productivity by…	17%
3.	More sales by…	20%
4.	Greater profitability by…	21%
5.	Less turnover in low-turn. industries by…	24%
6.	Less shrinkage by…	28%
7.	Fewer quality defects by…	40%
8.	Lower absenteeism by…	41%
9.	Fewer patient safety accidents by…	58%
10.	Less turnover in high-turn. industries by…	59%
11.	Fewer employee safety accidents by…	70%
12.	Outperformance of other entities by…	202%

Most Impressive Benefits

Consider the numbers in the table above to fully understand the impact of engagement. How do they relate to your specific industry and job title?

●	Which two are the most impressive? What if they were yours?
1.	
2.	

REAL MOTIVATION > TOTAL ENGAGEMENT > LEADERSHIP EXCELLENCE

Full Engagement HR Benefits

Think back to the incredible upsides regarding fully engaged employees. Our valued staff can both add value and reduce expenses in their various departments or teams while they are with us, and we hope they will be our partners for a long time.

Retention and churn rates are watched very closely by many Human Resources managers, as they can affect the company top and bottom lines. According to Dale Carnegie & Associates and Gallup, engaged personnel are less likely to look for other employment.

- Cost to replace an employee?
- Time to get a new employee fully trained?
- When engaged, 87% less likely to leave
- Looking for new job right now:
    - 37% of those fully engaged
    - 56% of those partially engaged
    - 73% of those actively disengaged

Staying Fully Staffed

Gaining and loosing employees is a regular trial for many businesses, though it does not have to be that way. Positive employee attitudes can help prevent lost staff members, and promote the hiring of people who are good corporate fits.

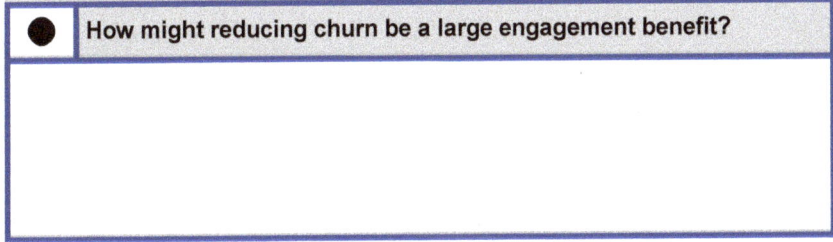

INSPIRED   David Benson Coaching

Shared Values Matter

Individuals are value-driven: we typically pursue activities, make friends, wed sweethearts, and join organizations whose values overlap with our own. We want the concepts, principles, beliefs, and moral constructs that are important to us to be important to others, or to at least be respected, maybe validated, by them if we differ.

Our values form a strong source of motivation. What we do in large part depends on the values we hold, and when our company holds to the same or similar, we sense pride and inspiration.

> *When your values are clear to you, making decisions becomes easier.*
> **—Roy E. Disney**

One of the values mentioned in the 2017 SOAW report (Gallup) reads, "[M]y associates or fellow employees are committed to doing quality work." When team members share values, engagement rises due to a sense of mutual inspiration for similar purposes or causes.

Our Values

List as many values as you can imagine in the box below, whether you hold those values or not. Consider possible values for your co-workers.

❶	**Which values do you think are most meaningful to your co-workers?**

_____   _____   _____

_____   _____   _____

_____   _____   _____

_____   _____   _____

_____   _____   _____

_____   _____   _____

Owned Values

Review the values recorded on the previous page. Which values do you consider to be most precious to you as a leader? Select the top three and place them in order of importance to you relevant to your work position.

■ How many of these top values are shared by people at your table?
1.
2.
3.

■ From the three, choose the ONE value that is most important to you.

INSPIRED

Communicative Congruence

Expressing our values, our vision, and similar weighty topics is momentous enough for us to be careful with the message delivery. Despite our care, we sometimes fail to accurately convey our meaning. Is it important that our actions support our words? How can we communicate consistently and unambiguously?

Based on two research papers in 1967, *Decoding of Inconsistent Communications* and *Inference of Attitudes from Nonverbal Communication in Two Channels*, Dr. Albert Mehrabian determined the impact of verbal and non-verbal communication cues.

Spoken Language = _____ %

Tone of Voice = _____ %

Body Language = _____ %

Communicative Congruence Examples

Much of humor is based on disconnects and confusion over contradictions in body language, tones of voice, and the language we use. Sarcasm is a great example of saying one thing but meaning another, and only non-verbal cues provide the true meaning.

 How do these examples demonstrate the need for congruence?

1. Verbal instructions do not match physical cues.
2. Tone of voice does not match verbal instructions.
3. "<u>I</u> <u>never</u> <u>said</u> <u>he</u> <u>was</u> <u>my</u> <u>son</u>."

> *Leadership is the capacity to translate vision into reality.*
> —Warren Bennis

Purposeful Congruence

Reflect on how we communicate with younger children: the mismatch in our vocabularies require us to more clearly emphasize the non-verbal aspects of communication. We exaggerate our volume, contrast, pacing, and pausing as we speak. We amplify our facial expressions and body movements, moving limbs around to make our point. We relax and enjoy!

Goldilocks and the Three Bears Exercise

Recall the fairy tale of Goldilocks and her reluctant hosts. How can we recount this story full of energy, emotion, and excitement, as if to a child? Mark the passage in preparation for delivery to the group.

> **Select two possible bullets to deliver to the other lab participants.**
>
> 1. Happy, little girl Goldilocks takes a long, tiring walk.
> 2. Dark, dank forest yields to a bright, cheerful meadow.
> 3. Porridge in the kitchen is too hot, too cold, just right.
> 4. Living room chairs are big, medium, and small.
> 5. Beds upstairs are too hard, too soft, just right.
> 6. Goldilocks upon waking is alarmed, frantic, relieved.

Congruence Story

Being congruent makes our communication more clear and believable.

> **In what specific situations at work can I be more congruent?**

INSPIRED

Commitment: Congruence Story

We have worked together this session on several distinct activities that contribute toward improved leadership. Revisiting each of them in some manner will lead to better mastery of the concepts and methods. Explicitly, please use your notes recorded above to deliver a Congruence Story to another person in a professional setting outside the lab before we meet for our next training session. Consider your own development or the benefit of a co-worker when deciding who to involve.

Prepare, Practice, and Report

Please prepare a Congruence Story activity to practice outside of training and then report back to the lab participants. Consider your own development or the benefit of a co-worker when deciding who to involve.

1	**Prepare details for your Congruence Story commitment.**

Congruence Story Title:

Who to Involve:

Why This Is Important:

What I Will Do:

How I Will Do It:

REAL MOTIVATION > TOTAL ENGAGEMENT > LEADERSHIP EXCELLENCE

Commitment Report Observations

As participants relate their commitment experiences, carefully watch their delivery. Note how they applied the principles we have discussed. Did they cover all aspects of the commitment? What specifically did they do well? Where were opportunities to coach for even more progress? What did you observe that you would like to appreciate, recognize, or adopt for yourself?

Observation Notes: Name, Compliment, Proof
1.
2.
3.
4.

Commitment Report Personal Debrief

Review the commitment report you just delivered. Consider your own input and feedback from the coach and fellow participants. List everything you did well, circling the one success that was most meaningful to you. Identify one challenge that will add the most leadership value to when improved.

All My Successes

_____

_____

_____

My One Greatest Challenge

_____

INSPIRED   David Benson Coaching

Realized Benefits

We train to realize our vision, to develop tools to reach our goals, to become more excellent, and to assist others in doing the same. Having performed the related objectives, consider how they have moved us closer to attaining our vision and mission.

- [x] Excellent
- [ ] Very good
- [ ] Good
- [ ] Average
- [ ] Poor

My Most Significant Benefit

Of all the benefits you may have experienced in this workshop, which one is the most significant for you, either professionally or personally? Why is this benefit essential to your leadership success?

_____

_____

_____

Benefitting Others

Our development serves to help those around us, our partners, teams, departments, and organizations. How will my most significant benefit impact those around me? Who in my circles of influence might also take advantage of this training to realize increased leadership success?

_____

_____

_____

_____

Motivational Speaking

Motivational? Of course! But our speaking engagements deliver so much more than the quickly fading warm fuzzy. Allow us to provide practical exercises and uplifting coaching as your keynote, break-out, or workshop speaker. Select from one of our many leadership excellence topics, or provide a custom subject to match your conference, convocation, or corporate retreat theme. Please speak with the coach about upcoming speaking opportunities for your organization.

Inspired Summary

Inspiration to continue development is essential to ripening motivation, the second key characteristic of leadership. Inspiration from underlying values takes us to the next level of engagement. As we understand key benefits of engagement, we desire to move ourselves and others towards the fully engaged level. We can do this by perfecting activities such as sharing values and congruence stories. We discussed three objectives:

1. Identify key benefits of full engagement
2. Explore values shared within organizations
3. Animate communications within teams

There are a number of questions to contemplate as we summarize this workshop. What concepts will result in the most positive impact if applied regularly? Which ones should be put into action right away? Why are those key? Which principles will make the most difference for improved leadership in your work situation? How can I most benefit the team that I am responsible for leading? In which area do I need to improve the most?

■ **What additional activities can help improve on these skills?**

■ **How will my relationships progress as I apply these concepts?**

REAL MOTIVATION > TOTAL ENGAGEMENT > LEADERSHIP EXCELLENCE

INSPIRED

Inspired Conclusion

Throw yourself into some work you believe in with all your heart, live for it, die for it, and you will find happiness that you had thought could never be yours.

—Dale Carnegie

Additional Notes

_____

_____

_____

_____

_____

_____

_____

_____

_____

_____

_____

_____

_____

_____

ENDORSED ENGAGEMENT
Forming Plans to Shape the Future

We want everyone on the bus, with us ...

ENDORSED

Becoming Endorsed

Leaders welcome the opinions and input of the people with whom they work. They look forward to hearing what others have to contribute, and embrace the chance to learn from them. They involve them in planning and related activities to ensure everyone is contributing.

Personal Insight: Endorsed

What does being endorsed mean to you? How does it relate to your current condition? In what ways will becoming more endorsed improve your situation?

_____

_____

_____

Strategy and Endorsed

No person is an island! It is tough to accomplish significant goals with a great team, and even more challenging alone. Gathering ideas is the start of creating plans to achieve our desired visions.

Sound Strategy ▸▸▸ **Endorsed** | **Precise** | **Refined**

Engagement and Endorsed

Our opinions and ideas are a part of us. When people and their ideas are accepted as worthwhile, even if they conflict with the status quo, their sense of value increases. Endorsed employees usually are grateful for the sense of belonging, receive it with open arms, and learn to pass it along to new employees and workers across functional teams.

ENDORSED

Training Objectives

Workshop objectives represent small goals designed to help us develop the leadership characteristic being deliberated. They provide both clear direction for our training activities, and a method for measuring successful application of the related content. They connect to the leadership skills we evaluated as part of our self-assessment at the start of our training.

As we diligently embrace these objectives, we will perceive positive changes in our performance and personality.

	Endorsed Training Objectives	♥
1.	Recognize engagement as being inclusive to encourage an attitude of teamwork	
2.	Respect and embolden varying opinions to solve problems through increased staff input	
3.	Align personal ambitions with group aims to enlarge our power to reach goals	

Linking to Engagement

Think back to the vision and mission for increasing total engagement that we considered at the beginning of the training. Reflect on how this characteristic relates to our desire to become more engaged.

=	How does becoming more endorsed support those aims? Why is increasing endorsement critical to becoming a successful leader?

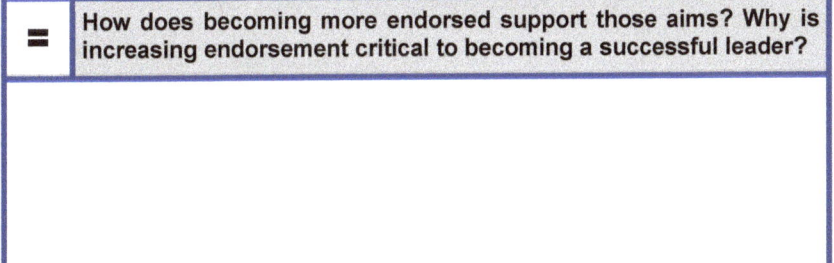

Productivity is never an accident. It is always the result of a commitment to excellence, intelligent planning, and focused effort.
—Paul J. Meyer

SOUND STRATEGY > TOTAL ENGAGEMENT > LEADERSHIP EXCELLENCE

Engagement Is Inclusive

According to a 2017 report by TINYpulse, staff members are not getting the attention they need. From just one year to the next, the number of employees expressing a strong sense of being valued, a cornerstone of engagement, dropped by over 16%.

This assuredly has led to a drop in engagement by those employees at their companies, perhaps even to significant increases in disengagement.

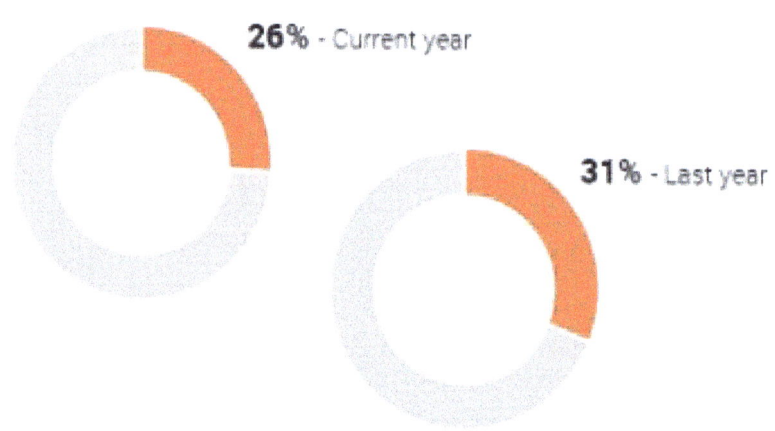

> **Who is responsible for these negative feelings? In what ways could these employees react to their perceived lack of value?**

Top Source of Engagement

So what is the solution to making our employees valued and keeping them engaged? According to the Dale Carnegie & Associates white paper titled *Emotional Drivers of Employee Engagement*, the answer is us.

- Immediate supervisors are the principal emotional driver in the workplace
- Explains 84% of how employees feel about their organizations
- Leaders create engagement in people
- Leaders decide how they will impact others

ENDORSED   David Benson Coaching

Respect and Embolden Opinions

Everyone has opinions, and usually on a lot of different topics. They are based on perception and fact, guided by experience, and colored by personal values. Forthright opinions are pieces of the people who hold them, and we should respect them like we would the person herself.

Some people hesitate to share their opinions. They feel unsafe, or unwelcome, or threatened by imposing personalities and abrasive temperaments. Maybe there is no outlet for sharing, or perhaps they have been rejected in a demeaning way in the past. The possibilities abound.

> ■ Compare incidents when your opinion was heard and when it was ignored. How did your engagement level change for each?

Great business advances can be gained by acting on opinions of our staff members, if we are willing to hear them. When we accept a person's intellectual input, we accept some of the best they have to offer.

> ■ What *crazy* ideas have changed our world for the better?

> *Every minute you spend in planning saves 10 minutes in execution; this gives you a 1,000 percent return on energy!*
> —Brian Tracy

ENDORSED

ROPE Opinion Model

Not every opinion is relevant, some might not be useful, and others might be contradictory to our own, but opinions from our people need to be heard and respected for engagement to flourish. This keeps communication lines open, and demonstrates we value our people. We should give them enough rope from which to hang their opinions.

R _____

O _____

P _____

E _____

=	How can the ROPE opinion model (receive, outlet, ponder, explain) overcome conflict? Increase engagement? Embolden the shy?

SOUND STRATEGY > TOTAL ENGAGEMENT > LEADERSHIP EXCELLENCE

ENDORSED

Align Personal and Organizational Goals

Allowing, encouraging, even expecting our team members to provide input to their individual and our group goals demonstrates that their opinions count. As leaders, we want them to have a chance to put their best foot forward every day. And we want them to attain positional and personal goals to maintain motivation and a sense of purpose.

As with personal and organizational values, flawless matches and seamless alignments are rarely reasonable. *Vive la différence!* And yet, greater engagement with all its benefits results when we are able to more fully align these ambitions.

• **How can individuals and the organization both achieve their goals? How does *WIIFM* figure into the discussion?**

SIRIUS Alignment Model

Compromise is a part of most every employment arrangement, with neither party receiving 100% of their wishes. When we honestly work towards our company goals, we can find ways to achieve our own, too.

S _____

I _____

R _____

I _____

US _____

= Why do we put our team first in the SIRIUS Alignment Model (speak, indicate, relevant, I, for US)? Where can we use it to align goals?

ENDORSED   David Benson Coaching

Commitment: ROPE Opinion Model

The quest for positive, exciting behavior change requires effort and stamina. It is for the strong-willed. In our workshop laboratory, we have explored activities contributing toward improved leadership. Continued practice and coaching will lead to mastery of the concepts and methods, ensuring solid, long-term results. Thank you for the authentic effort!

Prepare, Practice, and Report

Please prepare a ROPE Opinion Model to practice outside of training and then report back to the lab participants. Consider your own development or the benefit of a co-worker when deciding who to involve.

I — Prepare details for your ROPE Opinion Model commitment.

ROPE Opinion Model Title:

Who to Involve:

Why This Is Important:

What I Will Do:

How I Will Do It:

David Benson Coaching

ENDORSED

Commitment Report Observations

As participants relate their commitment experiences, carefully watch their delivery. Note how they applied the principles we have discussed. Did they cover all aspects of the commitment? What specifically did they do well? Where were opportunities to coach for even more progress? What did you observe that you would like to appreciate, recognize, or adopt for yourself?

Observation Notes: Name, Compliment, Proof
1.
2.
3.
4.

Commitment Report Personal Debrief

Review the commitment report you just delivered. Consider your own input and feedback from the coach and fellow participants. List everything you did well, circling the one success that was most meaningful to you. Identify one challenge that will add the most leadership value to when improved.

All My Successes

_____

_____

_____

My One Greatest Challenge

_____

ENDORSED

Realized Benefits

We train to realize our vision, to develop tools to reach our goals, to become more excellent, and to assist others in doing the same. Having performed the related objectives, consider how they have moved us closer to attaining our vision and mission.

My Most Significant Benefit

Of all the benefits you may have experienced in this workshop, which one is the most significant for you, either professionally or personally? Why is this benefit essential to your leadership success?

_____

_____

_____

Benefitting Others

Our development serves to help those around us, our partners, teams, departments, and organizations. How will my most significant benefit impact those around me? Who in my circles of influence might also take advantage of this training to realize increased leadership success?

_____

_____

_____

Transformation Project

As wise leaders know, training is an investment that can offer many kinds of returns, such as minimized employee turnover, increased sales, reduced expenses, amplified productivity, and greater customer satisfaction. Leadership training can provide some of the largest of returns on investment, especially to bottom line profitability. A Transformation Project is one way to demonstrate that ROI in hard numbers. Please speak with the coach about how this would be of use to your organization.

ENDORSED

Endorsed Summary

We must endorse different ideas and the people who generate them to better achieve our strategy, the third key characteristic of leadership. We engage ourselves and co-workers by welcoming everyone and their opinions to the planning process, and by aligning individual goals with corporate plans. Perfecting activities such as the ROPE Opinion model and the SIRIUS Alignment model will help us achieve our desired ends. We discussed three objectives:

1. Recognize engagement as being inclusive
2. Respect and embolden varying opinions
3. Align personal ambitions with group aims

There are a number of questions to contemplate as we summarize this workshop. What concepts will result in the most positive impact if applied regularly? Which ones should be put into action right away? Why are those key? Which principles will make the most difference for improved leadership in your work situation? How can I most benefit the team that I am responsible for leading? In which area do I need to improve the most?

■ What additional activities can help improve on these skills?

■ How will my relationships progress as I apply these concepts?

SOUND STRATEGY > TOTAL ENGAGEMENT > LEADERSHIP EXCELLENCE

Endorsed

Endorsed Conclusion

Mission first, men always.
—U.S. Military saying

Additional Notes

EMPOWERED ENGAGEMENT
Enabling the Push towards Distinction

If you love someone, set them free ...

EMPOWERED

Becoming Empowered

As we become more empowered, we grow in abilities and experience, taking on more responsibility and becoming more autonomous. We seek for higher quality relationships and outputs because we desire to express our best selves. Leaders encourage this in their colleagues, and celebrate when they succeed.

Personal Insight: Empowered

What does being empowered mean to you? How does it relate to your current condition? In what ways will becoming more empowered improve your situation?

_____

_____

_____

Quality and Empowered

Being empowered is the beginning of quality, the fourth key characteristic of leadership. We must be afforded resources and freedom to push ourselves towards superior work.

Pivotal Quality ➤➤➤ **Empowered** | **Discerning** | **Vigorous**

Engagement and Empowered

When people feel empowered, they are well on their way to full engagement. They know what they can achieve for themselves and their organization, and have shown competence to receive more responsibility. Empowered employees accept credit and blame for their efforts, realizing that they must stretch their abilities to achieve their audacious goals. Strong effort is accompanied by strong desire to assist.

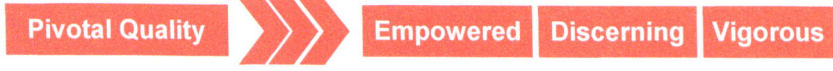

EMPOWERED

Training Objectives

Workshop objectives represent small goals designed to help us develop the leadership characteristic being deliberated. They provide both clear direction for our training activities, and a method for measuring successful application of the related content. They connect to the leadership skills we evaluated as part of our self-assessment at the start of our training.

As we diligently embrace these objectives, we will perceive positive changes in our performance and personality.

	Empowered Training Objectives	♥
1.	Boost autonomy in others to advance high quality work from subordinates	
2.	Organize processes for efficiency to see larger gains from resources	
3.	Celebrate achievements to delight in successes and prepare for more	

Linking to Engagement

Think back to the vision and mission for increasing total engagement that we considered at the beginning of the training. Reflect on how this characteristic relates to our desire to become more engaged.

=	How does becoming more empowered support those aims? Why is increasing empowerment critical to becoming a successful leader?

> *Treat employees like they make a difference and they will.*
> —Jim Goodnight

EMPOWERED

Boost Autonomy

As staff members become more engaged, they take their existing duties more seriously, and start to act like a unit CEO. They work towards goals with increasing independence. They are taking the next step toward total engagement. We can help them in the following ways.

- Remove routine reminders
- Give access to your calendar
- Lead, organize meetings
- Work on special projects
- Give title of assistant manager or similar
- Entrust with a discretionary budget
- Make key customer decisions
- Support them in their decisions
- Other ideas?

> *Accountability breeds response-ability.*
> —Stephen Covey

Maintain Autonomy

Increased autonomy can be difficult, even painful for some of our team members. They may resist the efforts we are making, or purposefully fail just so they can to return to a lower level of responsibility, one well within their previous comfort zone.

> ▲ **Discuss what actions team members employ to resist becoming more autonomous. Which actions have you actually experienced?**

Maintain Autonomy Exercise

Follow these steps to keep an empowered employee on track to considerable autonomy.

1. Set the meeting tone: time, location, smile
2. Praise for progress to date
3. Express confidence in abilities
4. Discuss why this is important. Benefits?
5. Commit to continuing autonomous actions
6. Confirm your ongoing support

> = **Practice maintaining autonomy with a peer coach. What was uncomfortable about the exercise? How did you help your staffer?**

EMPOWERED

Organization for Efficiency

How we approach our days and projects can make all the difference in the world. By organizing our processes and activities as part of our regular efforts, we ensure nothing is forgotten or lost, and that deadlines are met. We demonstrate that we take our work seriously.

Top-down Organization

Organizing our activities provides structure, strength, coordination among levels, and assurance that our actions are leading to progress for all.

- Mission and goals
    - Long-, mid-, short-term
- Daily routines
    - Stability, part of the *Who*
    - Anchors amid change
- Daily appointments supporting goals
    - Blocking time to combat distractions
- Daily tasks to support goals—to do list
    - Batching activities, certain times only
- Best practices, process documentation, etc.

- **Which area of organization could be the most improved? What changes would need to be made at your workplace?**

Time Blocking Activity

When we have an important assignment to fulfill, we often need to dedicate chunks of time to see it through. Blocking off time is designed to eliminate distractions as much as possible and focus on the task at hand.

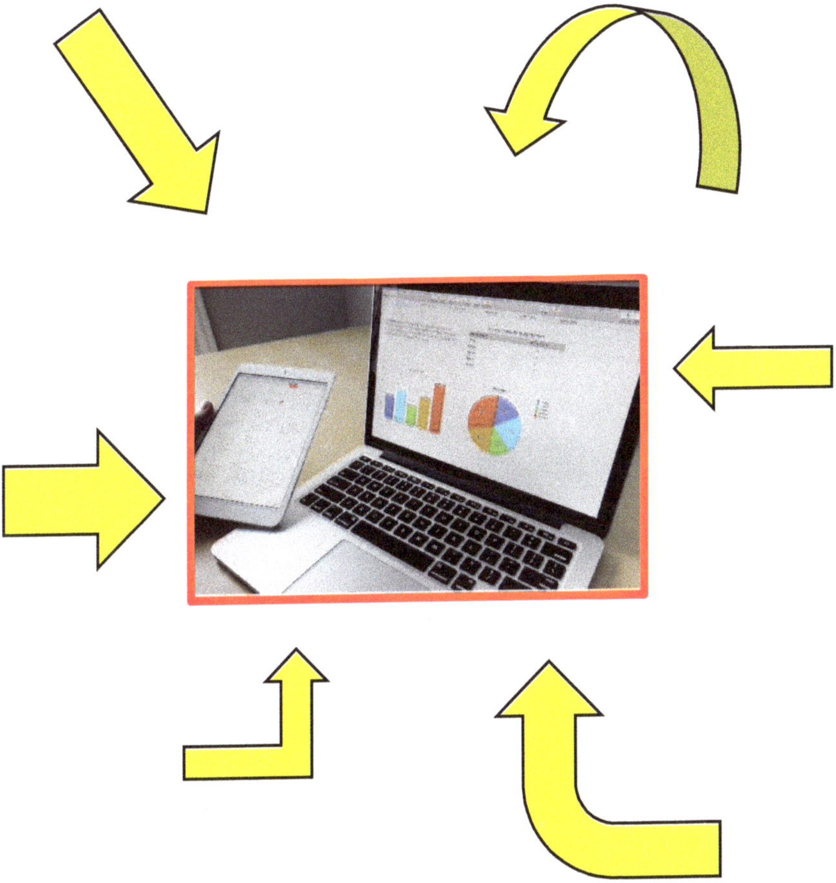

PIVOTAL QUALITY > TOTAL ENGAGEMENT > LEADERSHIP EXCELLENCE

Celebrate Successes

When the work is complete and we have accomplished much, it is time to celebrate and recognize our successes. This is vital to our ability to sustain a rigorous schedule of human labor over time. People need a chance to bask in the glow of a job well done, accept accolades, and prepare for whatever hurdles might be around the corner.

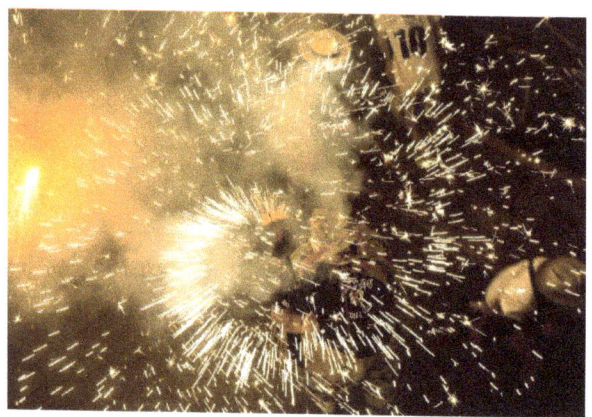

What makes for a good celebration at your office?

1. _____
2. _____
3. _____
4. _____
5. _____

> *Celebrate your successes.*
> *Find some humor in your failures.*
> —Sam Walton

Celebrate with a Purpose

In addition to relaxing and having fun, both important aspects of a business celebration, we can take advantage of celebrations to promote comraderies and engagement, and the desire for future wins. Take full advantage of a celebration by including these elements.

- Welcome newcomers to your team
    - Experience the fun side of work
    - Look forward to future successes
- Tell the campfire story and become a legend
    - Initial requirements
    - Problems along the way
    - Heroic efforts to win the day
- Recognize heroes
    - Be sensitive to personalities
    - Be genuine in praise
    - Offer amusing tokens in place of cash
- Invite everyone to the next victory

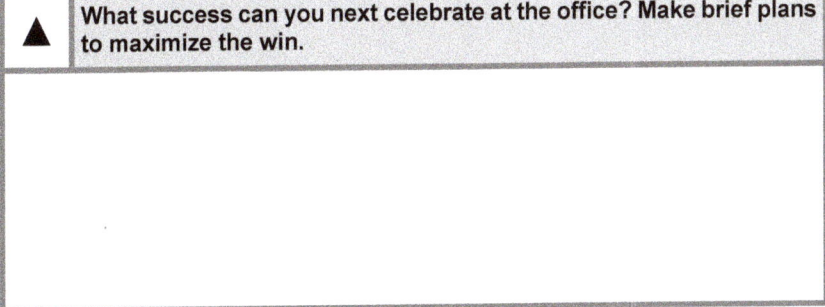

▲ What success can you next celebrate at the office? Make brief plans to maximize the win.

EMPOWERED   David Benson Coaching

Commitment: Maintain Autonomy

The quest for positive, exciting behavior change requires effort and stamina. It is for the strong-willed. In our workshop laboratory, we have explored activities contributing toward improved leadership. Continued practice and coaching will lead to mastery of the concepts and methods, ensuring solid, long-term results. Thank you for the authentic effort!

Prepare, Practice, and Report

Please prepare a Maintain Autonomy commitment to practice outside of training and then report back to the lab participants. Consider your own development or the benefit of a co-worker when deciding who to involve.

1	**Prepare details for your Maintain Autonomy commitment.**

Maintain Autonomy Title:

Who to Involve:

Why This Is Important:

What I Will Do:

How I Will Do It:

Commitment Report Observations

As participants relate their commitment experiences, carefully watch their delivery. Note how they applied the principles we have discussed. Did they cover all aspects of the commitment? What specifically did they do well? Where were opportunities to coach for even more progress? What did you observe that you would like to appreciate, recognize, or adopt for yourself?

Observation Notes: Name, Compliment, Proof
1.
2.
3.
4.

Commitment Report Personal Debrief

Review the commitment report you just delivered. Consider your own input and feedback from the coach and fellow participants. List everything you did well, circling the one success that was most meaningful to you. Identify one challenge that will add the most leadership value to when improved.

All My Successes

_____

_____

_____

My One Greatest Challenge

_____

EMPOWERED

Realized Benefits

We train to realize our vision, to develop tools to reach our goals, to become more excellent, and to assist others in doing the same. Having performed the related objectives, consider how they have moved us closer to attaining our vision and mission.

- [✓] Excellent
- [ ] Very good
- [ ] Good
- [ ] Average
- [ ] Poor

My Most Significant Benefit

Of all the benefits you may have experienced in this workshop, which one is the most significant for you, either professionally or personally? Why is this benefit essential to your leadership success?

_____

_____

_____

Benefitting Others

Our development serves to help those around us, our partners, teams, departments, and organizations. How will my most significant benefit impact those around me? Who in my circles of influence might also take advantage of this training to realize increased leadership success?

_____

_____

_____

_____

Impactful Facilitating

Already have a topic to present to your team and need someone to really make it engaging? Or just need an outside voice to lend credibility, add expertise, or support your own busy staff? We can add value and impact to your employee orientation, brain storming session, conflict resolution, problems solving exercise, or process improvement effort. Let our facilitation experience guide your teams to solid outcomes. Please speak with the coach if facilitating your next organizational event might be useful.

  **EMPOWERED**

Empowered Summary

Empowering people to get the job done is central to maturing quality, the fourth key characteristic of leadership. Empower ourselves and our co-workers, and engagement must shortly follow. As we boost autonomy in our staff, we find ways to overcome mediocrity and achieve greatness. We organize our efforts for maximum efficiency and celebrate our successes to guarantee even more of them. We discussed three objectives:

1. Boost autonomy in others
2. Organize processes for efficiency
3. Celebrate achievements

There are a number of questions to contemplate as we summarize this workshop. What concepts will result in the most positive impact if applied regularly? Which ones should be put into action right away? Why are those key? Which principles will make the most difference for improved leadership in your work situation? How can I most benefit the team that I am responsible for leading? In which area do I need to improve the most?

■ **What additional activities can help improve on these skills?**

■ **How will my relationships progress as I apply these concepts?**

Empowered Conclusion

Always blaze the better path instead of grooming the popular route. Always pursue greatness over mastering mediocrity.

—David Benson

Additional Notes

___
___
___
___
___
___
___
___
___
___
___
___
___
___
___

ENTHUSIASTIC ENGAGEMENT
Creating Unstoppable Passion in Others

Keep your friends close ...

ENTHUSIASTIC

Becoming Enthusiastic

With enthusiasm comes the penultimate culmination of engagement. Leaders who act enthusiastic become enthusiastic, and the emotion is typically contagious in the extreme. Elevated levels of enjoyment for and interest in the shared work become the norm.

Personal Insight: Enthusiasm

What does being enthusiastic mean to you? How does it relate to your current condition? In what ways will becoming more enthusiastic improve your situation?

_____

_____

_____

Altruism and Enthusiastic

Being enthusiastic is the beginning of altruism, the fifth key characteristic of leadership. More than mere interest, enthusiasm is marked by intensity and passion. We desire the contentment of those around us in earnest.

Engagement and Enthusiastic

When people feel enthusiastic, they are all but unstoppable. Their sense of worth becomes focused outward, turning to grasp how they can deeply impact those around them for the good. Enthusiastic employees act as salt to season their teams with a drive to help and serve. At this level of involvement in their companies, they expect to be models for others working toward full engagement.

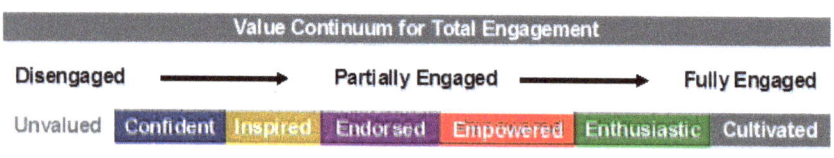

ENTHUSIASTIC

Training Objectives

Workshop objectives represent small goals designed to help us develop the leadership characteristic being deliberated. They provide both clear direction for our training activities, and a method for measuring successful application of the related content. They connect to the leadership skills we evaluated as part of our self-assessment at the start of our training.

As we diligently embrace these objectives, we will perceive positive changes in our performance and personality.

Enthusiastic Training Objectives	♥
1. Show interest with active communication to engender loyalty and support	
2. Reduce stress and worry to save expenses with a healthy staff	
3. Spread a culture of appreciation to shrink churn and strengthen outputs	

Linking to Engagement

Think back to the vision and mission for increasing total engagement that we considered at the beginning of the training. Reflect on how this characteristic relates to our desire to become more engaged.

=	How does becoming more enthusiastic support those aims? Why is increasing enthusiasm critical to becoming a successful leader?

> *Success consists of going from failure to failure without loss of enthusiasm.*
> —Winston Churchill

ENTHUSIASTIC

Show Interest

As employees or team members, the beginning of engagement is very introspective. Newly arrived at the organization, we are wary of our status and maybe unsure of our position. We look inward for self-confidence from education, past work history, and projects, while trying to accept our role in the company. The two questions from Gallup's 2017 *SOAW* report, Q02 (materials) and Q03 (best), that fit the Integrity Series require honesty and self-awareness to respond.

If this were to continue, our engagement level would be stunted, because we need to interact with others to develop certain skillsets and achieve our full potential. But we are also able to pursue the engagement of others. One way to help people become confident is to involve them in a simple conversation. We all like to talk about ourselves, and asking open-ended question ensures a high probability of hearing back in meaningful ways.

 How does showing interest in someone's personal life cause them to be enthusiastic in the workplace? When did you experience this?

Asking Questions

With a partner, take turns following previous suggestions, and these guidelines below.

> Start with a desire to learn about the person
> Ask open-ended questions
> Use the six interrogatives
> Listen carefully during the response
> Ask follow-up questions tied to the response
> Continue the response trail until exhausted

=	Which partner asked the most questions? How was that sustained? How did the listener feel interest from the questioner?

> *Being a good listener is absolutely critical to being a good leader; you have to listen to the people who are on the front line.*
> —Richard Branson

ENTHUSIASTIC   David Benson Coaching

Stress Effects

Stress, anxiety, worry. It is called by different names, but the effects are the same. Minor and sever health issues, absenteeism, lost productivity, frustration, anger, emotional and psychological problems, job loss – it seems as if stress can be a root cause for almost any diagnoses.

Stress has been called the "health epidemic of the 21st century" by the World Health Organization and is estimated to cost American businesses up to $300 billion a year.

businessnewsdaily.com

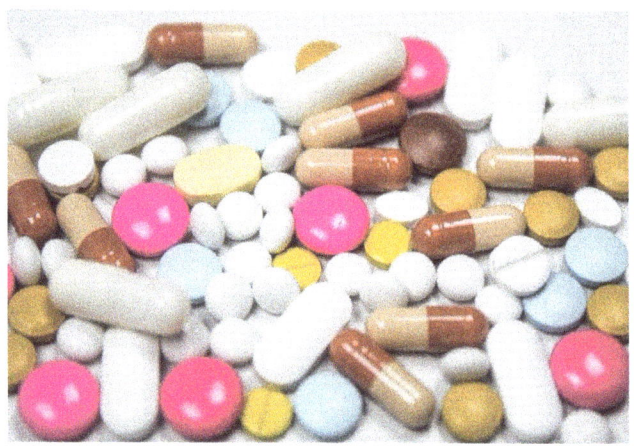

- **What contributes to stress in your work environment? How have you controlled or mitigated the effects of worry in the past?**

Reduce Stress

Anxiety, worry, and stress can weigh heavily on us at the workplace, especially with so many expectations. We are able to tackle the negative aspects of it through three main categories of stress busters. What specific methods can we use for each category?

- Take a healthy break from the stress
    - Exercise
    - Entertainment
    - Social networks
- Reason with the stress
    - Did my best, now move on
    - How much will I let this hurt me?
    - What's the worst outcome possible?
- Direct action against the stressor
    - Break it into small components
    - Make it a game
    - Celebrate small wins

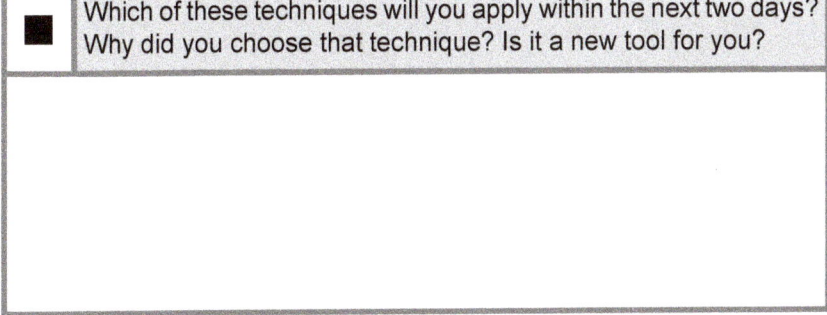

ENTHUSIASTIC

Spread Appreciation

We all wish to be appreciated, especially if it is a sincere thank you or congratulations for a job done well. What we do not *really* want to hear is silence, or some vague pleasantry about how *awesome* we happen to be. Contrary to popular opinion, no news is very often just *no news*, but our striving staff members deserve more than silence. If the only time we speak with them is to complain or point out a fault, how long will it take before they are avoiding us all together?

By the same token, what a difference to our culture we could achieve if we make it a point of always approaching people with good news. If this is true, they will be ever looking for us to stop by their workspace, hoping to catch a glimpse of us in the hallways, because we always bring sunshine and sweet summer rain to their almost certainly parched world.

=	List as many genuine compliments as you can for your partner in the training room. How would this be different for a co-worker?

> *Much of the stress that people feel doesn't come from having too much to do. It comes from not finishing what they've started.*
> —**David Allen**

TAPP Appreciation Model

Appreciation can be formal or less so, and sometimes being information has a greater impact, because it allows you to be more intimate and personal. The TAPP model for appreciation encourages just that: find an opportunity to *TAPP* someone on the shoulder and give them some appreciation using the guidelines below.

> ➢ Approach in a friendly, open manner
> ➢ Share the personality trait you admire
> ➢ Give some proof that what you say is true
>   - Specific as to time
>   - Specific as to activity

> *I hope people like me and appreciate me the way I am.*
> —**Steve Yzerman**

=	Use the TAPP Appreciation Model to compliment your partner. Which one trait and detailed proof will you use?

ENTHUSIASTIC

Commitment: TAPP Appreciation Model

The quest for positive, exciting behavior change requires effort and stamina. It is for the strong-willed. In our workshop laboratory, we have explored activities contributing toward improved leadership. Continued practice and coaching will lead to mastery of the concepts and methods, ensuring solid, long-term results. Thank you for the authentic effort!

Prepare, Practice, and Report

Please prepare a TAPP Appreciation Model activity to practice outside of training and then report back to the lab participants. Consider your own development or the benefit of a co-worker when deciding who to involve.

I	**Prepare details for your TAPP Appreciation Model commitment.**

TAPP Appreciation Model Title:

Who to Involve:

Why This Is Important:

What I Will Do:

How I Will Do It:

Commitment Report Observations

As participants relate their commitment experiences, carefully watch their delivery. Note how they applied the principles we have discussed. Did they cover all aspects of the commitment? What specifically did they do well? Where were opportunities to coach for even more progress? What did you observe that you would like to appreciate, recognize, or adopt for yourself?

Observation Notes: Name, Compliment, Proof
1.
2.
3.
4.

Commitment Report Personal Debrief

Review the commitment report you just delivered. Consider your own input and feedback from the coach and fellow participants. List everything you did well, circling the one success that was most meaningful to you. Identify one challenge that will add the most leadership value to when improved.

All My Successes

_____

_____

_____

My One Greatest Challenge

_____

ENTHUSIASTIC   David Benson Coaching

Realized Benefits

We train to realize our vision, to develop tools to reach our goals, to become more excellent, and to assist others in doing the same. Having performed the related objectives, consider how they have moved us closer to attaining our vision and mission.

- [✓] Excellent
- [ ] Very good
- [ ] Good
- [ ] Average
- [ ] Poor

My Most Significant Benefit

Of all the benefits you may have experienced in this workshop, which one is the most significant for you, either professionally or personally? Why is this benefit essential to your leadership success?

_____

_____

_____

Benefitting Others

Our development serves to help those around us, our partners, teams, departments, and organizations. How will my most significant benefit impact those around me? Who in my circles of influence might also take advantage of this training to realize increased leadership success?

_____

_____

_____

_____

Additional Training

We all know that excellence does not happen by accident. It takes dedication, persistence, and wisdom to make lasting, positive improvements to our leadership skillsets. This training event is one of many designed to develop our full potential as leaders. What other topics might benefit you or your organization? Please speak with the coach about recommendations for pursuing these very topics in more depth, or alternate topics that are critical to your ongoing success.

ENTHUSIASTIC

Enthusiastic Summary

Spreading enthusiasm for our projects and team members is central to maturing altruism, the fifth key characteristic of leadership. With sustained enthusiasm in ourselves and co-workers, engagement is nearly full. We become more enthusiastic in our engagement as we show interest in others, reduce our stress, and practice showing appreciation. We discussed three objectives:

1. Show interest with active communication
2. Reduce stress and worry
3. Spread a culture of appreciation

There are a number of questions to contemplate as we summarize this workshop. What concepts will result in the most positive impact if applied regularly? Which ones should be put into action right away? Why are those key? Which principles will make the most difference for improved leadership in your work situation? How can I most benefit the team that I am responsible for leading? In which area do I need to improve the most?

■ **What additional activities can help improve on these skills?**

■ **How will my relationships progress as I apply these concepts?**

ENTHUSIASTIC

Enthusiastic Conclusion

Everything is beautiful in its own way …
Everybody's beautiful in their own way …

—Ray Stevens

Additional Notes

CULTIVATED ENGAGEMENT
Promoting Habits to Preserve the Victory

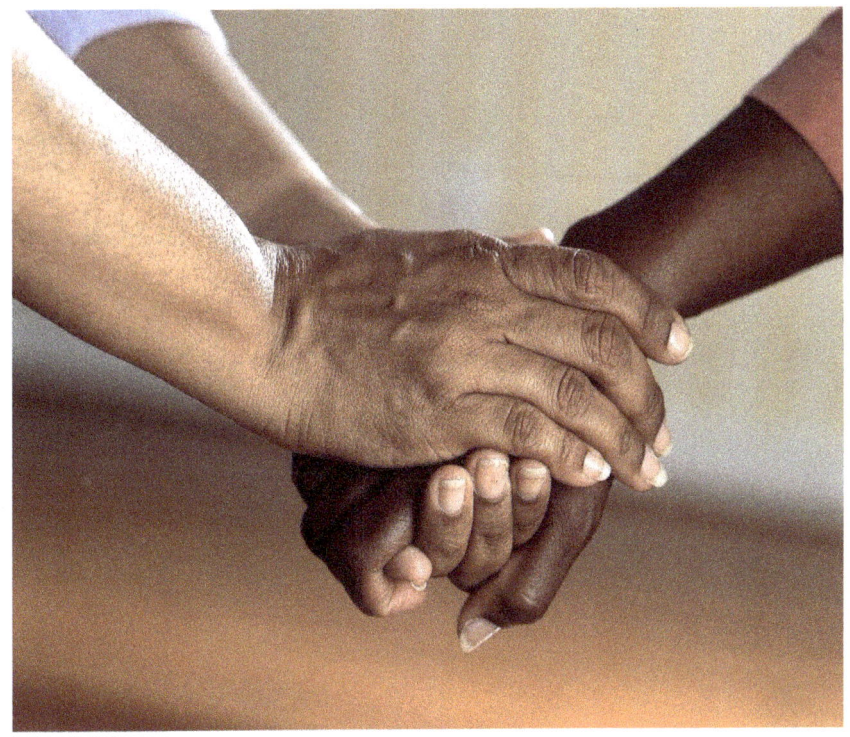

There is no crying in baseball ...

CULTIVATED

Becoming Cultivated

We cultivate skills when we gently nurture them and feed them until the young sprouts grow into strong plants and trees. Likewise, we cultivate a culture of engagement as we both seek to become engaged, and engage those around us.

Personal Insight: Cultivation

What does being cultivated mean to you? How does it relate to your current condition? In what ways will becoming more cultivated improve your situation?

_____

_____

_____

Coaching and Cultivated

Coaching should be performed with gentle hands and velvet gloves, not that we wish to avoid hard topics or difficult obstacles, but because we recognize how engagement depends on consistent, sympathetic inputs.

| Crucial Coaching | ⟫⟫⟫ | Cultivated | Guided | Mentored |

Engagement and Cultivated

When people are cultivated, they are nurtured and brought along only as quickly as they are ready to proceed. Coaches should be careful not to rush changes in behavior before their prodigy is prepared. Once employees feel cultivated, they are ready to continue the coaching process to achieve more integral levels of engagement. When the roots and branches are strong, fruit is produced in abundance.

Training Objectives

Workshop objectives represent small goals designed to help us develop the leadership characteristic being deliberated. They provide both clear direction for our training activities, and a method for measuring successful application of the related content. They connect to the leadership skills we evaluated as part of our self-assessment at the start of our training.

As we diligently embrace these objectives, we will perceive positive changes in our performance and personality.

	Cultivated Training Objectives	♥
1.	Convince our employees of their inherent value to reach full engagement	
2.	Host affirming performance reviews to sustain engagement	
3.	Cultivate habits of self- and peer coaching to encourage continuous improvement	

Linking to Engagement

Think back to the vision and mission for increasing total engagement that we considered at the beginning of the training. Reflect on how this characteristic relates to our desire to become more engaged.

=	How does becoming more cultivated support those aims? Why is increasing cultivation critical to becoming a successful leader?

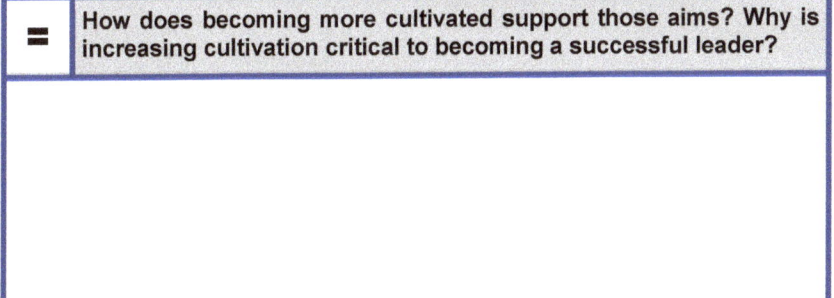

Engagement may have been optional in the past, but it's pretty much the whole game today.
—Gary Hamel

CULTIVATED   David Benson Coaching

Convinced of Their Value

A shepherd loves her sheep, a farmer loves her crops, a parent loves her children, and a leader loves her employees. We are so obviously valuable to each other that it sometimes seems odd to mention it. Start now to convince your staff members, or continue convincing them, that they are immensely valuable to you as a supervisor and to your organization. Be authentic and forthright in the expression, and they will reciprocate with thanks and excitement.

Convincing Actions

Whenever possible, engage in actions that will uplift and encourage our employees in any effort we wish to magnify. They will soon and nearly without fail become the super-valued team members you expect.

> ➤ Ask questions more than giving orders
> ➤ Allow freedom more than constraint
> ➤ Offer praise more than criticism
> ➤ Catch them doing good
> ➤ Speak well of them in all situations
> ➤ _____

Reach Full Engagement

List co-workers, especially team members under your supervision, for whom you would like to cultivate full engagement. Which ones have the most potential, or are in need of the most cultivation, or could really make a difference on your team? From our list of names, select one person to commit to cultivating within the next two days.

_____

_____

Cultivation Activities

Review the activities below that we have discussed to create engagement in our employees. Circle the one that you will use right away to start cultivating the employee selected above.

Greetings to Build Trust	Time Blocking
Memorable Moments	Celebrate Success
Share Values	Show Interest
Animate Conversations	Reduce Stress and Worry
ROPE Opinion Model	TAPP Appreciation Model
SIRIUS Alignment Model	Convince of Value
Boost Autonomy	Affirming Performance Reviews

CULTIVATED

Employee Performance Reviews

Traditional employee performance reviews have been rather hierarchal and one-sided: the manager or supervisor calls the staff member into her office, tells her what kind of job she has been doing for the last 12 months, gives her commands on where to improve, and then says goodbye before either of them has a chance to consider how unlikely anything worthwhile is to result from that encounter. (I recall just such a performance review early in my career.)

> *The big problems are where people don't realise they have one in the first place.*
> —W. Edwards Deming

This type of corrective performance review stands in stark contrast to the self-directing, affirming reviews engaging managers are able to hold with their engaged staff. While the corrective approach is all about identifying errors and insisting that they not happen again, the affirming approach focusses on the integrity, motivation, and strategy of the *reviewee*, as they align with the purposes and goals of the host company.

Perhaps one of the largest distinctions between these two types of reviews is the direction in which the participants are facing. The corrective review looks backwards, with the manager and employee figuratively looking in opposite directions. The affirming interview looks forward, with both people peering figuratively into the future side by side to seize improvements upon the current situation.

▲ | Discuss how to conduct a performance review (topics, manner of discussion, etc.) if your only purpose was to benefit your employee?

Affirming Performance Review

Use the table below to create the details for two types of performance reviews: the traditional, corrective approach to the review, and then the affirming, supportive, reassuring, and sustaining approach.

Topic	Corrective	Affirming
1.		
2.		
3.		
4.		
5.		
6.		
7.		

	When is your next scheduled performance review? What aspects of the affirming type are you able/willing to incorporate into it?

CRUCIAL COACHING > TOTAL ENGAGEMENT > LEADERSHIP EXCELLENCE

CULTIVATED

Self- and Peer and Coaching

Traditional coaching is hierarchal: a person with more experience or insight provides direction to a person with les of one or both. This is useful in many situations, including business. Peer coaching is when people at approximately the same experience level guide each other. Self-coaching is when we remember our training and make corrections on our own.

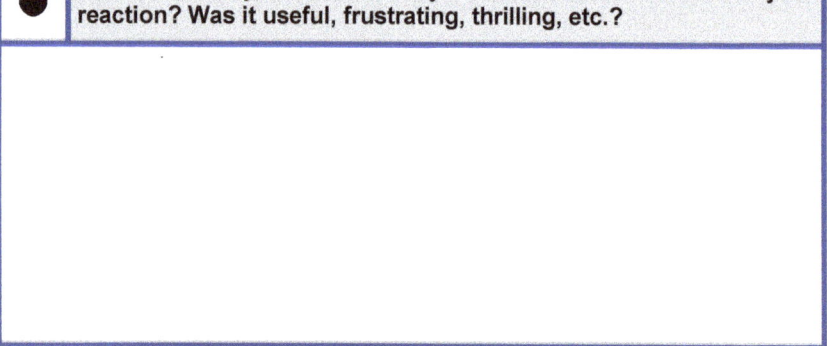

Recall when you successfully self-coached. What was your reaction? Was it useful, frustrating, thrilling, etc.?

CULTIVATED

Peer Coach a Memorable Moment

Use the page below to coach a Memorable Moment related by a partner. Follow the outline to ensure all points are properly delivered.

> **=** Use the Memorable Moment format to coach your partner. Then have your partner coach you on an M&M.

Memorable Moment (good, bad, or ugly as long as it impacts!):

Vivid Details (people, reason, situation, date, location, challenge:

Result (How did I act/react in the moment? Outcome?):

My Identity (How did I improve? What traits were strengthened?):

Apply Now (How can this help overcome a current challenge?):

> **I** Who are you? Would you rather act the coach, or deliver the M&M?

CRUCIAL COACHING > TOTAL ENGAGEMENT > LEADERSHIP EXCELLENCE   7.9

CULTIVATED
David Benson Coaching

Commitment: Peer Coaching

The quest for positive, exciting behavior change requires effort and stamina. It is for the strong-willed. In our workshop laboratory, we have explored activities contributing toward improved leadership. Continued practice and coaching will lead to mastery of the concepts and methods, ensuring solid, long-term results. Thank you for the authentic effort!

Prepare, Practice, and Report

Please prepare a Peer Coaching commitment to practice outside of training and then report back to the lab participants. Consider your own development or the benefit of a co-worker when deciding who to involve.

I | **Prepare details for your Peer Coaching commitment.**

Peer Coaching Title:

Who to Involve:

Why This Is Important:

What I Will Do:

How I Will Do It:

CRUCIAL COACHING > TOTAL ENGAGEMENT > LEADERSHIP EXCELLENCE

Commitment Report Observations

As participants relate their commitment experiences, carefully watch their delivery. Note how they applied the principles we have discussed. Did they cover all aspects of the commitment? What specifically did they do well? Where were opportunities to coach for even more progress? What did you observe that you would like to appreciate, recognize, or adopt for yourself?

Observation Notes: Name, Compliment, Proof
1.
2.
3.
4.

Commitment Report Personal Debrief

Review the commitment report you just delivered. Consider your own input and feedback from the coach and fellow participants. List everything you did well, circling the one success that was most meaningful to you. Identify one challenge that will add the most leadership value to when improved.

All My Successes

_____

_____

_____

My One Greatest Challenge

_____

CULTIVATED

Realized Benefits

We train to realize our vision, to develop tools to reach our goals, to become more excellent, and to assist others in doing the same. Having performed the related objectives, consider how they have moved us closer to attaining our vision and mission.

- [✓] Excellent
- [ ] Very good
- [ ] Good
- [ ] Average
- [ ] Poor

My Most Significant Benefit

Of all the benefits you may have experienced in this workshop, which one is the most significant for you, either professionally or personally? Why is this benefit essential to your leadership success?

_____

_____

_____

Benefitting Others

Our development serves to help those around us, our partners, teams, departments, and organizations. How will my most significant benefit impact those around me? Who in my circles of influence might also take advantage of this training to realize increased leadership success?

_____

_____

_____

_____

Executive Coaching

Determined to supercharge culture and obliterate obstacles? Enlist our coaching services to make a lasting impact for your organization. Participants are held accountable for developing the improved skills and new habits they desire, with guided follow-up to ensure success. Executive coaching is also available for individuals ready to take their leadership game to the next level. Please speak with the coach if about executive coaching for your members of your organization.

Cultivated Summary

Being available to provide guidance and feedback to eager staff members is central to maturing coaching, the sixth key characteristic of leadership. As we continue to coach our employees, we foster an ongoing culture of dedicated, fulfilling work. We can do this by perfecting activities such as convincing employees of their inherent value, hosting affirming performance reviews and engaging in self- and peer coaching. We discussed three objectives:

1. Convince employees of their value
2. Host affirming performance reviews
3. Cultivate habits of self- and peer coaching

There are a number of questions to contemplate as we summarize this workshop. What concepts will result in the most positive impact if applied regularly? Which ones should be put into action right away? Why are those key? Which principles will make the most difference for improved leadership in your work situation? How can I most benefit the team that I am responsible for leading? In which area do I need to improve the most?

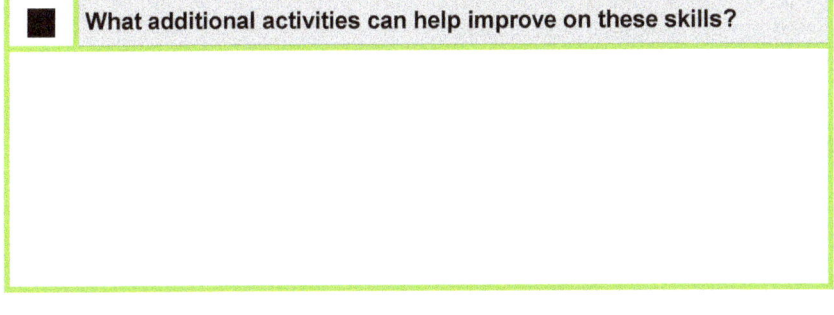

What additional activities can help improve on these skills?

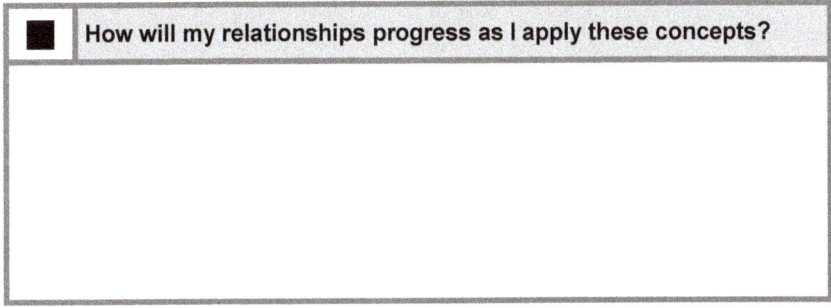

How will my relationships progress as I apply these concepts?

CULTIVATED

Cultivated Conclusion

If excellent players leave it all on the field, then excellent coaches leave it all on the players.

—David Benson

Additional Notes

_____
_____
_____
_____
_____
_____
_____
_____
_____
_____
_____
_____
_____
_____
_____
_____

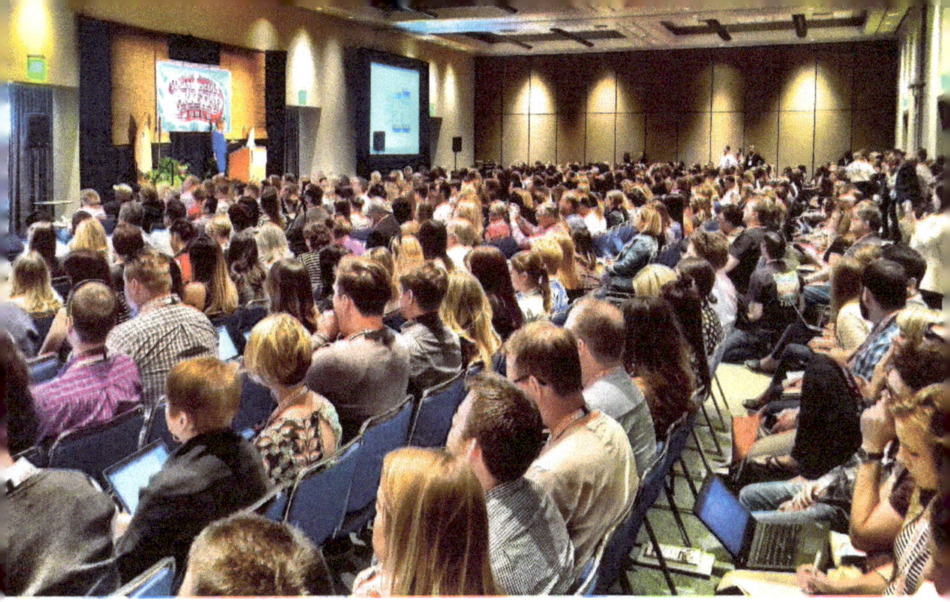

Dynamic Presentations Track
Crafting Optimal Conversations

_____

Participant Name

PRESENTATIONS

Leadership and Presentations

We have heard that the only constant in the universe is change, and the professional development world is no different. It seems new research is regularly leading to new models, techniques, and fads. Learners pursuing leadership excellence need only focus on enduring principles to succeed, aiming at clear, written, vibrant targets to measure progress.

 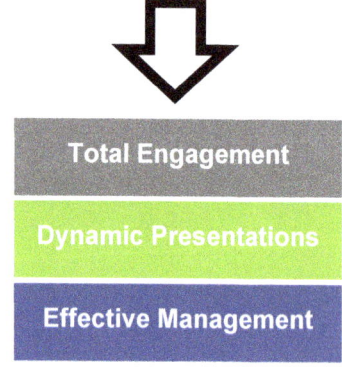

The abilities to present concepts and plans, to speak to groups, and to be believable are crucial to the success of those who wish to lead. We become more successful at presenting as we become increasingly comfortable with ourselves, our material, and our audiences. Progression along the comfort continuum starts with being genuine, then stirring, precise, discerning, persuasive, and finally guided.

As part of the Leadership Excellence course, this Dynamic Presentations track will investigate how to apply the six leadership characteristics to those speaking in public.

A presenter's sense of comfort culminates as they are able to persuade audiences to take action, and to accept guidance from an experienced colleague. It is only then that they can assertively accept opportunities to speak to different audiences.

Introducing Presentations

The word presentation for our purposes is a general term that describes the process of delivering a message or topic to an audience in a particular environment. The message might be basic information, or an emotional appeal to convince people that something is proper or just, or ultimately a persuasive petition combining facts with feelings to drive an audience to action.

The audience could be a single person, a friend or colleague, or it might be a small group of co-workers on a close-knit team. The audience may well be a group of strangers, industry specialists or potential customers. It conceivably could consist of a huge group of people, part of a corporate retreat or a convention keynote audience. The possibilities are numerous.

The environment of the presentation can vary as well, from an impersonal phone call, to a discussion at a boardroom table, to a formal presentation with electronic media delivered standing on a podium.

Wherever you are tasked to speak, write, or otherwise communicate with other people, our skills as dynamic presenters come into play. Communication in this way is one of the most imperative skills for a leader to develop, being lively, productive, and compelling for our audiences.

Presentations Self-Assessment

Please frankly assess yourself for each leadership skill below based on your current situation using a scale from 0-10 (*never* to *always*). Rate your abilities before training, then again after the training is complete.

Leadership Skills to Measure	Before	After	+ / -
1. I am at ease when delivering a presentation.			
2. I connect with my audiences when speaking.			
3. My attitude matches the intent of communications.			
4. I am passionate about the topics I discuss.			
5. I make impactful, memorable presentations.			
6. When I speak, my message is organized and clear.			
7. I convey complicated topics in clear and coherent ways.			
8. I handle stressful situations with tactful responses.			
9. I command the attention of my listeners.			
10. My communication is persuasive to others.			
11. I contribute to my own success with self-coaching.			
12. I encourage peers to continuously improve.			
Assessment Totals (120 points max.)			

Once the presentations training has ended and the above assessment complete, please identify the most significant value, benefit, or gain for:

13. You as an individual, professionally, personally, or otherwise.

_____

_____

14. Your organization, business, community, or other relationships.

_____

_____

Personality Change

The phrase *you are what you eat* may be true to some degree, but the more important realization is that we are what we experience. We are what we think, feel, express, and do. Our personality is the intricate blend of our emotional and behavioral characteristics or traits that uniquely distinguish us from each other. We form our personality by our thoughts and actions.

Improvement only occurs when we make a decision to shift our emotions and behavior in some direction. Changing either without the other is insufficient, and though excellence can be difficult, it can be achieved when we work towards it.

$$PC = EC \times IC \times BC$$

Transforming Presentations

Think of the many possible benefits you might realize through this dynamic presentations training. What do you want to improve about yourself as an individual or a leader? How about in your teams, or in your work situation generally? What admirable qualities, habits, or processes do you see elsewhere that you would like to adopt for yourself? What would you need to get out of this training to make it completely and utterly worthwhile?

_____

_____

_____

_____

_____

_____

_____

_____

PRESENTATIONS

Becoming Dynamic

Communication is complex. Even the simplest of messages can be difficult to accurately convey to another person. Add distance, group size, and extenuating circumstances, and communicating can be downright tough. As we become dynamic presenters, we increase the chances that our vital leadership messages will be received, understood, and accepted.

Identity

We wear many hats in many divergent situations. For the purposes of this training, determine your primary title, position, or role in your organization.

I	**Please record <u>who</u> you are for our training purposes.**

Vision

An inspiring statement of purpose or motivation describes our future, ideal situation. Briefly state your vision of a more dynamic, persuasive leader.

●	**Please record <u>why</u> you want to make presentations more dynamic.**

Mission

A single, ambitious, overarching goal defines what we will do to realize our vision. This has more detail, covering all aspects of our work. Subordinate milestones and tasks support it. Briefly state your presentations mission.

↪	**Please record <u>what</u> you will do to achieve your presentations vision.**

GENUINE PRESENTATIONS
Finding the Courage to Be Authentic

The genuine article…

GENUINE

Becoming Genuine

As we become more genuine, we are increasingly sincere and comfortable with who we are. We shed pretenses and stand sincerely in the place of our true selves. We realize that we can be confident with our own contributions, for we add value through our unique gifts and talents.

Personal Insight: Genuine

What does being genuine mean to you? How does it relate to our opening activity/discussion? In what ways will becoming more genuine improve your current situation?

_____

_____

_____

Integrity and Genuine

Becoming more genuine continues our journey towards increased integrity, the first key characteristic of leadership. The boldness from our confident beginnings allows us to express ourselves in authentic, natural ways. This honestly about ourselves engenders honesty in all interactions.

Presentations and Genuine

When we feel genuine, our communications cannot help but be more genuine as well. We express ourselves sincerely, adding ease and a relaxed demeanor to our dialog, fostering connections with our audiences.

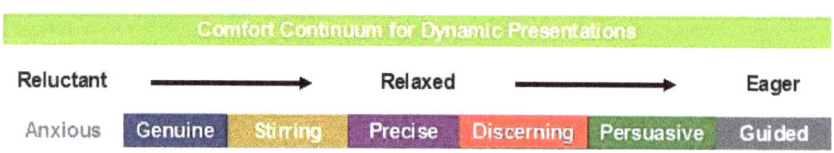

  GENUINE

Training Objectives

Workshop objectives represent small goals designed to help us develop the leadership characteristic being deliberated. They provide both clear direction for our training activities, and a method for measuring successful application of the related content. They connect to the leadership skills we evaluated as part of our self-assessment at the start of our training.

As we diligently embrace these objectives, we will perceive positive changes in our performance and personality.

Genuine Training Objectives	♥
1. Experience immediate speaking success by delivering a presentation from familiar material	
2. Conquer common presentation anxieties to strengthen delivery comfort	
3. Build rapport with the audience to increase influence	

Linking to Presentations

Think back to the vision and mission for increasing dynamic presentations that we considered at the beginning of the training. Reflect on how this characteristic relates to our desire to become more dynamic.

=	How does becoming more genuine support those aims? Why is increasing genuineness critical to becoming a successful leader?

> *A genuine leader is not a searcher for consensus, but a molder of consensus.*
> —Martin Luther King, Jr.

Familiar Material

There are certainly things that we can identify as being objectively true, measured in impartial or absolute terms. Yet even those items can be subject to personal, individual interpretation. Recall the parable of the blind men meeting an elephant for the first time from different perspectives, all with great variation, and yet all true. In this way, it is arguable that every experience is personal. We experience the world through individual filters.

Speak from Within

While being open to other opinions, we each relate our version of events most genuinely. We understand it best and most thoroughly.

- Our experiences are personal
- When relevant, they are equally valid
- We add the most value when we contribute that which *only we* can

Our Owned Perspective

When we speak about what we already know, we are most able to be genuine with our audience. It matters little if they know the same material or not, for we provide our own take on it, our personal approach that can only originate from us.

Sources of Familiar Material

We possess a wealth of topics to pull from when speaking, and a wealth of variations and new topics to last a lifetime.

- First-person experiences
    - Know these best
    - Relate to existing issue or skill
- Researched topics
    - Make it our own
    - Become an expert
- Second-person sources

GENUINE

Conquer Anxieties

Spiders, heights, failure, death, and public speaking – we all have fears that hold us back. Why is speaking to large or small groups, sometimes just one other person, at times intimidating?

_____

_____

Initial Antidotes

Knowing the topic goes a long way to overcoming the stress of speaking, but there are many other actions we can take to reduce our stress.

- Self-talk: know topic, excited, positive
- Focus on the content, add details
- Focus on the audience, add value
- Trust ourselves, trust our audience
- Reducing stress techniques: 2 categories

▲ **Which method of conquering anxiety will you try next? Why?**

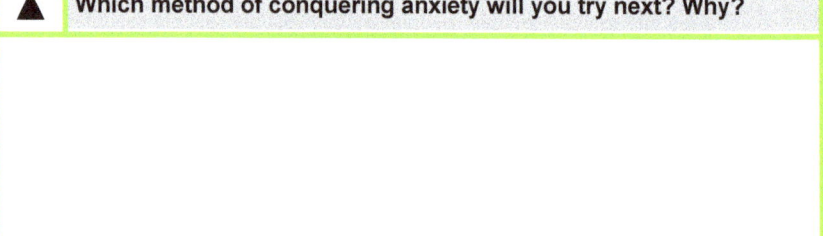

The best way to conquer stage fright is to know what you're talking about.
—Michael Mescon

Options for Conquering

When we find something that works, we tend to stick with it. There is comfort in the familiarity, though the same approach may not work in different situations. Developing more tools will ensure our ability to overcome in those differing situations.

Determine a familiar topic to present in the lab. It might be one you pick yourself, or one given you by the coach. Apply the options below to practice overcoming presentation anxiety.

▲ **Use self-talk (know topic, excited, positive) to help overcome anxieties. How useful is this approach for you?**

▲ **Focus on the content (add details) to help overcome anxieties. How useful is this approach for you?**

▲ **Focus on the audience (add value) to help overcome anxieties. How useful is this approach for you?**

GENUINE

Build Rapport

Rarely are we nervous about conversing with people we already know well. The engaged relationship smooths over all interactions. Building a connection with our audiences allows us to speak with them as if we were old friends. Like first impressions, affinity can be built rather quickly.

Constructing Empathy and Sympathy with an Audience

There are many methods for making a connection with our audience. Having multiple tools available makes us more versatile in the various circumstances that might arrive. Focus on being in the moment and enjoying the audience as you know they will enjoy you.

> ➢ Advance research for understanding
> ➢ Greet and mingle before event
> ➢ Refer to audience members by name
> ➢ Thank audience for allowing me to come
> ➢ Offer compliments during presentation

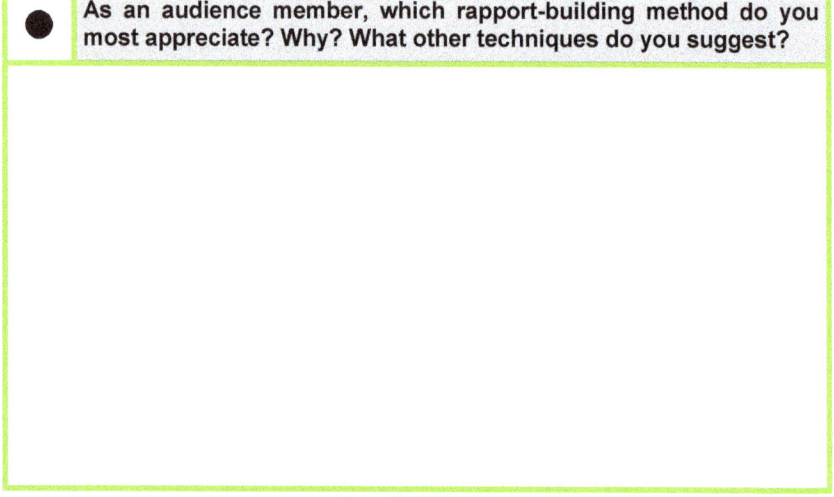

● As an audience member, which rapport-building method do you most appreciate? Why? What other techniques do you suggest?

GENUINE

Putting it All Together

Now is the time to put everything together. Review the objectives laid out at the beginning of this workshop, and the related principles we have discussed. Identify the topics that really hit home for you, those that will have an impact on future presentations. There may be subjects with which you are already comfortable when speaking to an audience, and others that might need a little more practice to make them powerful allies in developing your delivery skills. Incorporate them into this presentation.

Genuine Presentation Instructions

Relate a short, personal success story that is very familiar to you. Topics from professional settings are best. Include notes on how you will apply the principles reviewed in this workshop.

- Topic: personal success story
- Time Limit: 2 minutes
- Incorporate training objectives:
    - Familiar material
    - Conquer anxieties
    - Build rapport

GENUINE

Commitment: Genuine Presentation

The quest for positive, exciting behavior change requires effort and stamina. It is for the strong-willed. In our workshop laboratory, we have explored activities contributing toward improved leadership. Continued practice and coaching will lead to mastery of the concepts and methods, ensuring solid, long-term results. Thank you for the authentic effort!

Prepare, Practice, and Report

Please prepare a Genuine Presentation to practice outside of training and then report back to the lab participants. Consider your own development or the benefit of a co-worker when deciding who to involve.

I — Prepare details for your Genuine Presentations commitment.

Presentation Title:

Details of Familiar Material:

Conquer Anxieties:

Build Rapport:

Commitment Report Observations

As participants relate their commitment experiences, carefully watch their delivery. Note how they applied the principles we have discussed. Did they cover all aspects of the commitment? What specifically did they do well? Where were opportunities to coach for even more progress? What did you observe that you would like to appreciate, recognize, or adopt for yourself?

Observation Notes: Name, Compliment, Proof
1.
2.
3.
4.

Commitment Report Personal Debrief

Review the commitment report you just delivered. Consider your own input and feedback from the coach and fellow participants. List everything you did well, circling the one success that was most meaningful to you. Identify one challenge that will add the most leadership value to when improved.

All My Successes

_____

_____

_____

My One Greatest Challenge

_____

GENUINE   David Benson Coaching

Realized Benefits

We train to realize our vision, to develop tools to reach our goals, to become more excellent, and to assist others in doing the same. Having performed the related objectives, consider how they have moved us closer to attaining our vision and mission.

- [✓] Excellent
- [ ] Very good
- [ ] Good
- [ ] Average
- [ ] Poor

My Most Significant Benefit

Of all the benefits you may have experienced in this workshop, which one is the most significant for you, either professionally or personally? Why is this benefit essential to your leadership success?

_____

_____

_____

Benefitting Others

Our development serves to help those around us, our partners, teams, departments, and organizations. How will my most significant benefit impact those around me? Who in my circles of influence might also take advantage of this training to realize increased leadership success?

_____

_____

_____

_____

Helping Others Succeed

When we have a personal or professional breakthrough, we instinctively look to share the benefit with those close to us. We want them to succeed as well. Think of team members, colleagues, industry friends, even local neighbors who are seeking to improve their current situation, to become more excellent leaders. Who among them would be responsive to leadership training? Please speak with the coach about how to involve them in this very same or subsequent training events.

Genuine Summary

Becoming genuine allows us to move beyond our confident foundation and grow in personal integrity, the first key characteristic of leadership. We become more comfortable speaking our mind, confronting our shortcomings, and perusing what is most valuable to us. As we practice dynamic presentations, we become better leaders and impact the progress of others at the same time. We discussed three objectives:

1. Deliver presentations from familiar material
2. Conquer common presentation anxieties
3. Build rapport with the audience

There are a number of questions to contemplate as we summarize this workshop. What concepts will result in the most positive impact if applied regularly? Which ones should you put into action right away? Why are those key? Which principles will make the most difference for improved leadership in your work situation? How can I most benefit the team that I am responsible for leading? In which area do I need to improve the most?

■	**How will speaking genuinely impact your team members?**

■	**Pinpoint a specific situation where these techniques can be used right away. Why that situation?**

GENUINE

Genuine Conclusion

You need to believe in yourself and what you do. Be tenacious and genuine.
—Christian Louboutin

Additional Notes

_____

_____

_____

_____

_____

_____

_____

_____

_____

_____

_____

_____

_____

_____

_____

_____

STIRRING PRESENTATIONS
Rousing Audiences through Natural Fervor

Why are you always stirring the pot …

STIRRING

Becoming Stirring

A stirring experience rouses, causes great emotion, and pushes audiences to the edge of initial activity. We present for different reasons, and though some may seem elementary, the passion we convey through words, voice, and body language will cement our purpose every time.

Personal Insight: Stirring

What does being stirring mean to you? How does it relate to your current condition? In what ways will becoming more stirring improve your situation?

_____

_____

_____

Motivation and Stirring

Stirring builds on our inspiration to motivate us to action, moving us to take the next steps towards our vision. This second key characteristic of leadership can be fickle, requiring regular reminders and refreshers. Motivation becomes a routine part of our daily walk.

Presentations and Stirring

Being a stirring speaker affects increases our own motivation, and that of our audiences. This is useful at the most basic level to convince an audience of our seriousness on a given topic. It is also utile when prompting an audience to take action, in that the see the vision that we already have in mind.

Training Objectives

Workshop objectives represent small goals designed to help us develop the leadership characteristic being deliberated. They provide both clear direction for our training activities, and a method for measuring successful application of the related content. They connect to the leadership skills we evaluated as part of our self-assessment at the start of our training.

As we diligently embrace these objectives, we will perceive positive changes in our performance and personality.

Stirring Training Objectives	♥
1. Harmonize presentation purposes with delivery to exhibit credibility	
2. Convey passion for our presentation topics to thrill audiences	
3. Stretch boundaries to expand speaking capabilities and comfort	

Linking to Presentations

Think back to the vision and mission for increasing dynamic presentations that we considered at the beginning of the training. Reflect on how this characteristic relates to our desire to become more dynamic.

> **How does becoming more stirring support those aims? Why is increasing excitement critical to becoming a successful leader?**

The past speaks to us in a thousand voices, warning and comforting, animating and stirring to action.
—Felix Adler

Presentation Purposes

Before we shower our audiences with passionate pleas, we must determine the *why* behind our presentation. This will permit us to measure an enthusiasm appropriate to our topic, and stir our listeners.

Speech Categories

All presentations or speeches may be categorized into four purposes. Passive spectators become active participants as we move down the spectrum, and aspects of each can blend into the others, especially if we decide to add value to the experience.

- Entertain – audience enjoys
- Inform – audience understands
- Convince – audience feels
- Persuade – audience moves

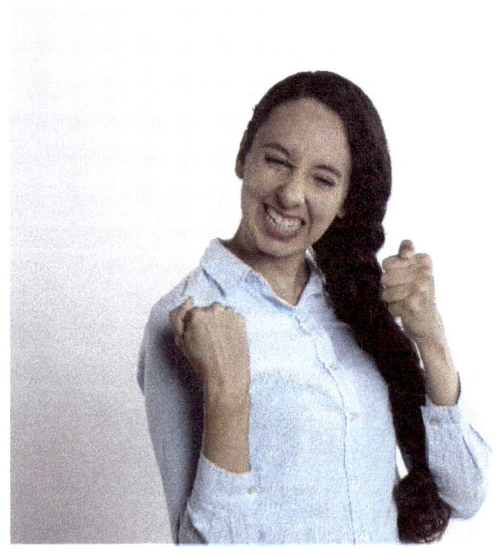

Harmonize Presentation Delivery

Determining the purpose for our presentations is key to accomplishing our goals for each. The purpose will help shape our preparation, how we connect to the audience, and the intensity we decide to deliver.

Aspects of Harmony

We can harmonize our presentations in these ways to ensure we make the impact we intend.

- Preparation – what? How much?
- Audience – biases, desires, background
- Presenter credibility
    - Speak at their level, shorthand
    - Become one of them
- Energy level

 Demonstrate how to harmonize delivery with intent for the first three types of presentations for both of the audience types below.

Trainee in New Position:

Experienced Vendor:

STIRRING

Convey Passion

Our passion drives us and motivates from the inside. When we know someone closely, we have a good idea about what gives them purpose because we have seen their motivation over time. Most of our listeners may not know us well enough to possess this insight. We must convince them of our passion through exterior clues: voice, face, and full body.

Practice Congruence

Cultural cues tend to be widely known, but narrowly expressed. We can become more convincing, adding to our authenticity and genuineness, as we provide those cues.

- Surprise
- Satisfaction
- Impatience
- Elation
- Frustration
- _____

> Prepare to deliver an example of passion for different emotions. What did you learn about yourself from this exercise?

Passion is energy. Feel the power that comes from focusing on what excites you.
—**Oprah Winfrey**

Stretch Boundaries

Just like an unused rubber band becomes brittle, or untested muscles fail, so does our ability to express ourselves in professional settings atrophy when not exercised. Our delivery skills can be stretched by applying techniques we may only rarely use.

- Spoken language:
    - Imagery
    - Superlatives
    - Colors, bright, flashy
- Voice:
    - Tone, sound effects
    - Inflection, pitch
    - Pacing, pauses
    - Volume, silence
- Body language:
    - Arms, legs, hands, feet
    - Posture
    - Contortions
    - All with purpose

- _____

STIRRING

Expand Speaking Capabilities

We can apply all of the techniques to our own speech, but it is even more difficult to make use of them with words from another author. Let us stretch ourselves to see how many techniques we can use on the following short excerpt from Herman Melville's *Moby Dick*. Prepare your delivery by marking the text with personal notes to guide your actions.

There are certain queer times and occasions in this strange mixed affair we call life when a man takes this whole universe for a vast practical joke, though the wit thereof he but dimly discerns, and more than suspects that the joke is at nobody's expense but his own.

● What was difficult about this activity? Where can these skills be utilized for increased effect at your workplace? What obstacles should we prepare to overcome?

Putting it All Together

Now is the time to put everything together. Review the objectives laid out at the beginning of this workshop, and the related principles we have discussed. Identify the topics that really hit home for you, those that will have an impact on future presentations. There may be subjects with which you are already comfortable when speaking to an audience, and others that might need a little more practice to make them powerful allies in developing your delivery skills. Incorporate them into this presentation.

Stirring Presentation Instructions

Relate a short, personal story full of emotion and activity that is very familiar to you. Topics from professional settings are best. Relive the experience with energy, congruence, and passion. Include notes on how you will apply the principles reviewed in this workshop.

- ➢ Topic: personal story full of emotion, activity
- ➢ Time Limit: 2 minutes
- ➢ Incorporate training objectives:
    - o Harmonize purpose and delivery
    - o Convey passion
    - o Stretch boundaries

Commitment: Stirring Presentation

The quest for positive, exciting behavior change requires effort and stamina. It is for the strong-willed. In our workshop laboratory, we have explored activities contributing toward improved leadership. Continued practice and coaching will lead to mastery of the concepts and methods, ensuring solid, long-term results. Thank you for the authentic effort!

Prepare, Practice, and Report

Please prepare a Stirring Presentation to practice outside of training and then report back to the lab participants. Consider your own development or the benefit of a co-worker when deciding who to involve.

1	**Prepare details for your Stirring Presentations commitment.**

Presentation Title:

Harmonize Purpose and Delivery:

Convey Passion:

Stretch Boundaries:

  **STIRRING**

Commitment Report Observations

As participants relate their commitment experiences, carefully watch their delivery. Note how they applied the principles we have discussed. Did they cover all aspects of the commitment? What specifically did they do well? Where were opportunities to coach for even more progress? What did you observe that you would like to appreciate, recognize, or adopt for yourself?

Observation Notes: Name, Compliment, Proof
1.
2.
3.
4.

Commitment Report Personal Debrief

Review the commitment report you just delivered. Consider your own input and feedback from the coach and fellow participants. List everything you did well, circling the one success that was most meaningful to you. Identify one challenge that will add the most leadership value to when improved.

All My Successes

_____

_____

_____

My One Greatest Challenge

_____

Realized Benefits

We train to realize our vision, to develop tools to reach our goals, to become more excellent, and to assist others in doing the same. Having performed the related objectives, consider how they have moved us closer to attaining our vision and mission.

- ☑ Excellent
- ☐ Very good
- ☐ Good
- ☐ Average
- ☐ Poor

My Most Significant Benefit
Of all the benefits you may have experienced in this workshop, which one is the most significant for you, either professionally or personally? Why is this benefit essential to your leadership success?

_____

_____

_____

Benefitting Others
Our development serves to help those around us, our partners, teams, departments, and organizations. How will my most significant benefit impact those around me? Who in my circles of influence might also take advantage of this training to realize increased leadership success?

_____

_____

_____

_____

Motivational Speaking

Motivational? Of course! But our speaking engagements deliver so much more than the quickly fading warm fuzzy. Allow us to provide practical exercises and uplifting coaching as your keynote, break-out, or workshop speaker. Select from one of our many leadership excellence topics, or provide a custom subject to match your conference, convocation, or corporate retreat theme. Please speak with the coach about upcoming speaking opportunities for your organization.

  STIRRING

Stirring Summary

Becoming a stirring orator moves us past inspiration and convinces us and others of our purpose, our motivation for pursing a course of action. Leaders convey passion and purpose, and motivate those around them. As we practice dynamic presentations, we become better leaders and impact the progress of others at the same time. We discussed three objectives:

1. Harmonize purpose and delivery
2. Convey passion
3. Stretch boundaries

There are a number of questions to contemplate as we summarize this workshop. What concepts will result in the most positive impact if applied regularly? Which ones should you put into action right away? Why are those key? Which principles will make the most difference for improved leadership in your work situation? How can I most benefit the team that I am responsible for leading? In which area do I need to improve the most?

■ **How will stirring your audience impact your team members?**

■ **Imagine that passion is suddenly infused in every organizational communication. What will be different? Why is this desirable?**

REAL MOTIVATION > DYNAMIC PRESENTATIONS > LEADERSHIP EXCELLENCE

STIRRING

Stirring Conclusion

Twenty years from now you will be more disappointed by the things that you didn't do than by the ones you did do.

—Mark Twain

Additional Notes

_____

_____

_____

_____

_____

_____

_____

_____

_____

_____

_____

_____

_____

_____

_____

PRECISE PRESENTATIONS
Giving the Heart a Particular Advantage

Robin Hood, William Tell, and Katniss Everdeen ...

PRECISE

Becoming Precise

Leaders know that planning for the future is the only way to achieve their visions. They spend valuable time and resources developing strategies to match the passion of their visions, recognizing that complete and exacting goals make the vision possible.

Personal Insight: Precise

What does being precise mean to you? How does it relate to your current condition? In what ways will becoming more precise improve your situation?

_____

_____

_____

Strategy and Precise

Our strategy, the third leadership characteristic, is the audacious plan that achieves our vision. The more precise our goals for the future, the more likely we are to achieve our mission. Once we have endorsed the ideas of our team members, it is time to set out specific goals.

Presentations and Precise

Our presentation comfort level increases as we add energy to our delivery, and then corroborate that enthusiasm with well-structured and thoughtful preparation. The organization of our presentations makes a big difference as we communicate with those we wish to influence.

PRECISE

Training Objectives

Workshop objectives represent small goals designed to help us develop the leadership characteristic being deliberated. They provide both clear direction for our training activities, and a method for measuring successful application of the related content. They connect to the leadership skills we evaluated as part of our self-assessment at the start of our training.

As we diligently embrace these objectives, we will perceive positive changes in our performance and personality.

	Precise Training Objectives	♥
1.	Couple particulars with passion to increase our standing as a speaker	
2.	Project planned posture and tenor to convey deliberate thoughtfulness	
3.	Speak with structure and lucidity to add impact	

Linking to Presentations

Think back to the vision and mission for increasing dynamic presentations that we considered at the beginning of the training. Reflect on how this characteristic relates to our desire to become more dynamic.

=	How does becoming more precise support those aims? Why is increasing preciseness critical to becoming a successful leader?

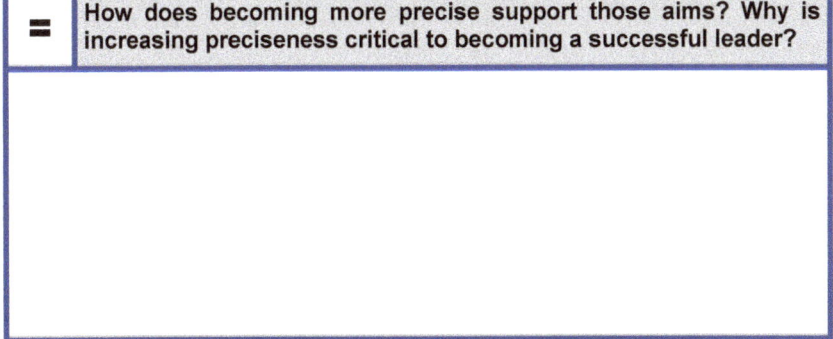

A good orator is pointed and impassioned.
—Marcus Cicero

PRECISE

Couple Particulars with Passion

Passion is vital for success in any weighty undertaking because it drives us forward. Being precise is vital for a different reason: it gives us a path to follow, a route that will direct us past distractions, around pitfalls, and through challenges in a deliberate manner.

As crucial as emotions are in communicating purpose or vision, they are often discounted when unaccompanied by deliberate plans. Our feelings and our intellect – the heart and the brain – must combine to provide credible, dynamic presentations.

Precision Areas

We can be precise and organized in four main areas of our presentations.

- Deliberate physical delivery:
    - Choice of words
    - Voice control
    - Presence
- Complete structure
- Organized content
- Thorough preparation

PRECISE

Planned Posture and Tenor

How we look and what we do impact the reception we receive from our audience. Having a friendly and open demeanor is the foundation. Adding calm, confident poise brings authority to our stirring expressions. Our verbal tenor contributes in like manner to how we are perceived.

Presenting Ourselves

We can plan our visual and auditory delivery just like the organization and content of our presentation.

- Eye contact
- Powerful stance: feet, hips, shoulders
- Hands calmly by our sides
- Purposeful movement around the podium
- Safe house
- Clear, crisp voice
- Bonus: the warm-up, physical and verbal

> Practice each action above. Which will be the most difficult to master? Which will have the greatest bearing on your next delivery?

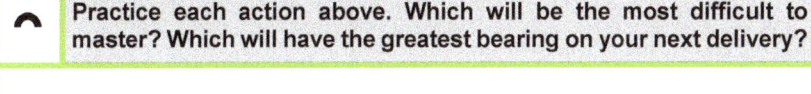

A strong confident person can rule the room with knowledge, personal style, attitude and great posture.
—Cindy Ann Peterson

PRECISE

Speak with Structure

The way we begin and end our presentations, and how the book-ends relate to the middle, will add power and influence. They may even be more memorable. Plan for these aspects of the delivery to be thorough.

- Opening up
    - Compliment, story
    - Quote, question
    - Statement, current event, joke?
- Related to the message
- Summary
- Closing down
    - Quotation, testimonial
    - Repeat points, review process
    - Call to action, emotional appeal

▲ Given a brief topic, select an opening and a closing to relate to the message. Was one easier than the other? If so, why?

PRECISE

Speak with Lucidity

Organizing our material is crucial to a relaxing and well-received presentation. In addition to including openings and closings, we should order our content so that it makes sense within the body of the presentation, and makes it simple for our audience to follow.

> - Limit topic scope and main ideas
> - Keep it simple: vocabulary, concepts
> - Introduce main ideas (tell them)
> - Logical flow of main ideas (tell them)
> - Exhibits to emphasize
> - Summarize main ideas (tell them)

Analyze the coach's example. Which technique added the most value to the presentation?

PRECISE

Speak with Exhibits

Some say a picture is worth a thousand words. If that is true, then an actual three dimensional object must be worth at least that much. Sometimes all it takes to solidify a concepts is a simple object that we can hold up to our audience and say, "See. Like this." Exhibits can add the extra juice to knock our presentation out of the park.

Types of Exhibits

The objects we use to convey meaning conform to no specific format, size, texture, or composition. Use whatever it takes to clarify your message.

Exhibit Guidelines

Exhibits betray their purpose when they take over the presentation, block the speaker, or distract the audience from the rest of the message. With the power of exhibits to illustrate comes an equal responsibility to keep them domesticated.

- ➢ Presenter remains the message
- ➢ Keep speaker in sight
- ➢ Set exhibit aside when not in use
- ➢ _____

Putting it All Together

Now is the time to put everything together. Review the objectives laid out at the beginning of this workshop, and the related principles we have discussed. Identify the topics that really hit home for you, those that will have an impact on future presentations. There may be subjects with which you are already comfortable when speaking to an audience, and others that might need a little more practice to make them powerful allies in developing your delivery skills. Incorporate them into this presentation.

Precise Presentation Instructions

Teach a skill, process, policy, or other activity that you practice at work to the lab participants so that they understand it well. Limit the main points to no more than four, and prepare an exhibit (slides welcome) to emphasize the main points. Topics from professional settings are best. Include notes on how you will apply the principles reviewed in this workshop.

- Topic: teach a skill, process, policy, activity
- Time Limit: 3 minutes
- Incorporate training objectives:
  - Particulars with passion
  - Posture and tenor
  - Structure and lucidity

PRECISE

Commitment: Precise Presentation

The quest for positive, exciting behavior change requires effort and stamina. It is for the strong-willed. In our workshop laboratory, we have explored activities contributing toward improved leadership. Continued practice and coaching will lead to mastery of the concepts and methods, ensuring solid, long-term results. Thank you for the authentic effort!

Prepare, Practice, and Report

Please prepare a Precise Presentation to practice outside of training and then report back to the lab participants. Consider your own development or the benefit of a co-worker when deciding who to involve.

I — Prepare details for your Precise Presentations commitment.

Presentation Title:

Particulars with Passion:

Posture and Tenor:

Structure and Lucidity:

PRECISE

Commitment Report Observations

As participants relate their commitment experiences, carefully watch their delivery. Note how they applied the principles we have discussed. Did they cover all aspects of the commitment? What specifically did they do well? Where were opportunities to coach for even more progress? What did you observe that you would like to appreciate, recognize, or adopt for yourself?

Observation Notes: Name, Compliment, Proof
1.
2.
3.
4.

Commitment Report Personal Debrief

Review the commitment report you just delivered. Consider your own input and feedback from the coach and fellow participants. List everything you did well, circling the one success that was most meaningful to you. Identify one challenge that will add the most leadership value to when improved.

All My Successes

_____

_____

_____

My One Greatest Challenge

_____

PRECISE

Realized Benefits

We train to realize our vision, to develop tools to reach our goals, to become more excellent, and to assist others in doing the same. Having performed the related objectives, consider how they have moved us closer to attaining our vision and mission.

☑ Excellent
☐ Very good
☐ Good
☐ Average
☐ Poor

My Most Significant Benefit

Of all the benefits you may have experienced in this workshop, which one is the most significant for you, either professionally or personally? Why is this benefit essential to your leadership success?

_____

_____

_____

Benefitting Others

Our development serves to help those around us, our partners, teams, departments, and organizations. How will my most significant benefit impact those around me? Who in my circles of influence might also take advantage of this training to realize increased leadership success?

_____

_____

_____

_____

Transformation Project

As wise leaders know, training is an investment that can offer many kinds of returns, such as minimized employee turnover, increased sales, reduced expenses, amplified productivity, and greater customer satisfaction. Leadership training can provide some of the largest of returns on investment, especially to bottom line profitability. A Transformation Project is one way to demonstrate that ROI in hard numbers. Please speak with the coach about how this would be of use to your organization.

PRECISE

Precise Summary

Becoming precise lends more credibility to our presentations while outlining a road map for us to follow. Our strategy, the third key characteristic of leadership, is laid out as we reveal where we are going and how we will get there. As we practice dynamic presentations, we become better leaders and impact the progress of others at the same time. We discussed three objectives:

1. Couple passion with particulars
2. Project planned posture and tenor
3. Speak with structure and lucidity

There are a number of questions to contemplate as we summarize this workshop. What concepts will result in the most positive impact if applied regularly? Which ones should you put into action right away? Why are those key? Which principles will make the most difference for improved leadership in your work situation? How can I most benefit the team that I am responsible for leading? In which area do I need to improve the most?

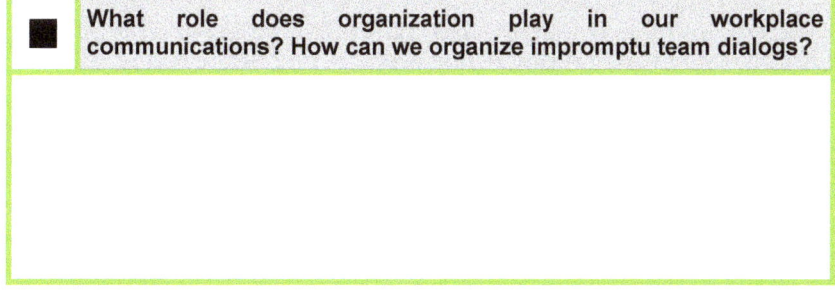

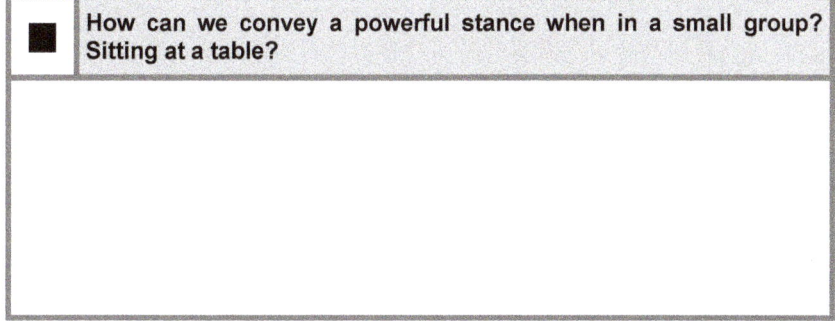

SOUND STRATEGY > DYNAMIC PRESENTATIONS > LEADERSHIP EXCELLENCE

PRECISE

Precise Conclusion

Organizing is what you do before you do something, so that when you do it, it is not all mixed up.

—A. A. Milne

Additional Notes

_____
_____
_____
_____
_____
_____
_____
_____
_____
_____
_____
_____
_____
_____
_____
_____

DISCERNING PRESENTATIONS
Injecting Judgement into Our Performance

Judge not according to the appearance …

DISCERNING

Becoming Discerning

Discernment is the display of good judgment. As we become more discerning, we are able to accurately assess the form and function of our presentations, and the influence they have on their recipients. This leads to increasingly superior outcomes and to personal and group discussions of higher quality.

Personal Insight: Discerning

What does being discerning mean to you? How does it relate to your current condition? In what ways will becoming more discerning improve your situation?

_____

_____

_____

Quality and Discerning

Our ability to evaluate our own performance affords corrections towards exertions of higher quality, the fourth key characteristic of leadership. We navigate the path towards goal attainment with wisdom and distinction.

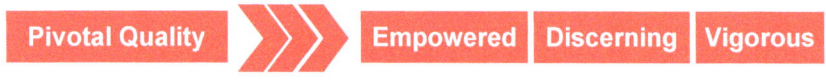

Presentations and Discerning

With clear organization and precision, we take the next step in our presentations journey toward high quality delivery. We channel our intellectual and attitudinal might to provide the best communication we can. And with that effort, we become more at ease in the spotlight.

DISCERNING

Training Objectives

Workshop objectives represent small goals designed to help us develop the leadership characteristic being deliberated. They provide both clear direction for our training activities, and a method for measuring successful application of the related content. They connect to the leadership skills we evaluated as part of our self-assessment at the start of our training.

As we diligently embrace these objectives, we will perceive positive changes in our performance and personality.

	Discerning Training Objectives	♥
1.	Draw on various forms of proof to support claims	
2.	Simplify complicated topics to aid understanding	
3.	Handle stressful situations with tactful responses to maintain composure and authority	

Linking to Presentations

Think back to the vision and mission for increasing dynamic presentations that we considered at the beginning of the training. Reflect on how this characteristic relates to our desire to become more dynamic.

=	**How does becoming more discerning support those aims? Why is increasing discernment critical to becoming a successful leader?**

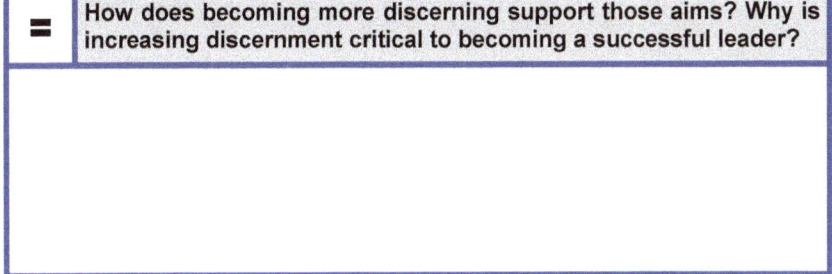

The human brain starts working the moment you are born and never stops until you stand up to speak in public.
—George Jessel

DISCERNING

Proof to Support Claims

Evidence types can vary widely based on the industry under consideration. The law might expect direct or circumstantial evidence, while the field of history might demand first- versus second-hand accounts. As we support claims in our presentations, judgement will dictate the best approach.

Forms of Evidence

We are able to support our claims with a variety of types of evidence. The proof we choose depends on our audience, our claim, and the category of presentation we are making.

- Statistical: facts, observation, objective
- Testimony: witness accounts, judgement
- Anecdotal: demos, examples
- Analogy: comparisons

> Which forms of proof are best suited for different audiences? Which form do we typically rely on to make our point? How would using an assortment of proof types affect our presentational influence?

Judging Reactions

Whether casual or formal, presentations are used as instruments to convey extra value beyond mute communiques. The active, human element allows for greater understanding and effectiveness. Our message comes alive as we interact with our audience.

The interactive component necessitates being able to discern how the give and take is progressing. Am I being clear? Is my team receiving the message I intend to deliver? Are we moving in the same direction?

Signs of Understanding

There are a number of clues by which we can we tell if our audience is receiving the same message we are sending, or if we have missed the mark with our efforts.

- Visible reactions
    - Head nods or shakes
    - Smiles/eye contact or distress
    - Attentive or distracted
    - _____
- Audible reactions
    - Clapping/laughter or mumbling
    - Discussion or silence
    - Movement of chairs, equipment
    - _____

Discerning

Simplify Complicated Topics

At times we are challenged to present complicated, intricate information to our listeners. Some audiences may be prepared for such complex material, while others may be completely overwhelmed. Keeping our content simple without dumbing it down is an art perfected through patient experience.

The Simplicity Challenge

When faced with complicated content, making advanced provisions to assist a perplexed audience pays rich dividends.

- ➢ Napoleon's Corporal
- ➢ Explain technical terms
- ➢ Analogies, then backup analogies
- ➢ Ask questions to determine understanding
- ➢ Respond to questions for clarification
- ➢ _____

=	Convey a short experience to your partner, asking questions to determine understanding. What variations did you try?

> *The ability to simplify means to eliminate the unnecessary so that the necessary may speak*
> —Hans Hofmann

Analogies Practice

Analogies are types of arguments that point out similarities between two things. They compare these two very different items in order to understand one or both of them more fully. An unfamiliar, sometimes complicated, and most likely confusing concept or object is likened to a second concept or object that is familiar, often simple, and certainly more easily understood. The juxtaposition of the one helps reveal the meaning, purpose, or notion of the other.

The ability to relate a foreign topic to another that is more meaningful to your audience is a very useful tool for the presenter. Practice creating analogies, across different industries and environments, allows one to make use of the tool at will. It can also be quite entertaining.

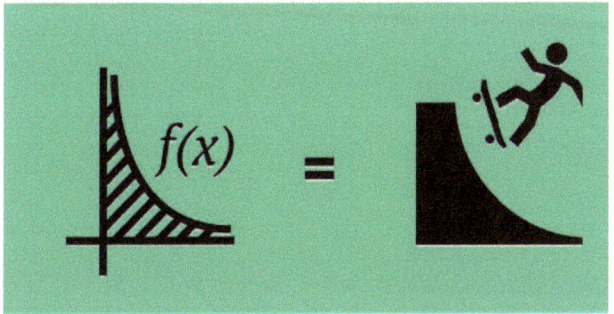

> ● **Practice analogies as simple explanations of complex data. Are we able to draw on three separate contexts to explain our topic? Can we construct analogies on the fly?**

DISCERNING

Tactful Responses

When feedback from our audience becomes confrontational, aggressive, or even combative, we gain the opportunity of exhibiting patience, self-control, and discernment to identify root causes and suitable solutions. Our role is to promote the original intent of our presentation, while resolving concerns for the benefit of all onlookers. This is our chance to shine!

- ➢ Listen to respect and understand
- ➢ Rephrase to confirm and clarify
- ➢ Thank without grading or grade equally
- ➢ Align comment with presentation theme
- ➢ Respond, or promise to respond offline
- ➢ Confirm helpfulness of response

▲ Practice providing tactful responses to scenarios. What step in the process most demands a discerning approach? How does this exercise relate to the *quality* leadership characteristic?

Putting it All Together

Now is the time to put everything together. Review the objectives laid out at the beginning of this workshop, and the related principles we have discussed. Identify the topics that really hit home for you, those that will have an impact on future presentations. There may be subjects with which you are already comfortable when speaking to an audience, and others that might need a little more practice to make them powerful allies in developing your delivery skills. Incorporate them into this presentation.

Discerning Presentation Instructions

Describe some positive characteristics of your organization, department, or team. Provide proof to support your claims. Be ready to tactfully respond to combative feedback. Topics from professional settings are best. Include notes on how you will apply the principles reviewed in this workshop.

- Topic: favorable aspects of your company
- Time Limit: 4 minutes
- Incorporate training objectives:
    - Draw on proof to support claims
    - Simplify complicated topics
    - Handle stressful situations with tact

DISCERNING

Commitment: Discerning Presentation

The quest for positive, exciting behavior change requires effort and stamina. It is for the strong-willed. In our workshop laboratory, we have explored activities contributing toward improved leadership. Continued practice and coaching will lead to mastery of the concepts and methods, ensuring solid, long-term results. Thank you for the authentic effort!

Prepare, Practice, and Report

Please prepare a Discerning Presentation to practice outside of training and then report back to the lab participants. Consider your own development or the benefit of a co-worker when deciding who to involve.

I | **Prepare details for your Discerning Presentations commitment.**

Presentation Title:

Evidence Based Support:

Simplify:

Tactful Response:

DISCERNING

Commitment Report Observations

As participants relate their commitment experiences, carefully watch their delivery. Note how they applied the principles we have discussed. Did they cover all aspects of the commitment? What specifically did they do well? Where were opportunities to coach for even more progress? What did you observe that you would like to appreciate, recognize, or adopt for yourself?

Observation Notes: Name, Compliment, Proof
1.
2.
3.
4.

Commitment Report Personal Debrief

Review the commitment report you just delivered. Consider your own input and feedback from the coach and fellow participants. List everything you did well, circling the one success that was most meaningful to you. Identify one challenge that will add the most leadership value to when improved.

All My Successes

_____

_____

_____

My One Greatest Challenge

_____

DISCERNING

Realized Benefits

We train to realize our vision, to develop tools to reach our goals, to become more excellent, and to assist others in doing the same. Having performed the related objectives, consider how they have moved us closer to attaining our vision and mission.

- [✓] Excellent
- [ ] Very good
- [ ] Good
- [ ] Average
- [ ] Poor

My Most Significant Benefit

Of all the benefits you may have experienced in this workshop, which one is the most significant for you, either professionally or personally? Why is this benefit essential to your leadership success?

_____

_____

_____

Benefitting Others

Our development serves to help those around us, our partners, teams, departments, and organizations. How will my most significant benefit impact those around me? Who in my circles of influence might also take advantage of this training to realize increased leadership success?

_____

_____

_____

_____

Impactful Facilitating

Already have a topic to present to your team and need someone to really make it engaging? Or just need an outside voice to lend credibility, add expertise, or support your own busy staff? We can add value and impact to your employee orientation, brain storming session, conflict resolution, problems solving exercise, or process improvement effort. Let our facilitation experience guide your teams to solid outcomes. Please speak with the coach if facilitating your next organizational event might be useful.

DISCERNING

Discerning Summary

Becoming discerning demands effort and patience, for being able to evaluate your presentation and its influence on the audience is no mean feat. It is a leg on the pathway to elevated quality, and demonstrations and proposals of great worth result. As we practice dynamic presentations, we become better leaders and impact the progress of others at the same time. We discussed three objectives:

1. Use proof to support claims
2. Simplify complicated topics
3. Handle stressful situations with tact

There are a number of questions to contemplate as we summarize this workshop. What concepts will result in the most positive impact if applied regularly? Which ones should you put into action right away? Why are those key? Which principles will make the most difference for improved leadership in your work situation? How can I most benefit the team that I am responsible for leading? In which area do I need to improve the most?

> ■ **How can we make habitual use of evidence in our presentations? What will be the biggest obstacle to that end?**

> ■ **In what situations might we resist simplifying presentation topics? Justify the decision with supporting proof.**

PIVOTAL QUALITY > DYNAMIC PRESENTATIONS > LEADERSHIP EXCELLENCE

DISCERNING

Discerning Conclusion

Judgement comes from experience, and experience comes from bad judgement.

—Simon Bolivar

Additional Notes

PERSUASIVE PRESENTATIONS
Speaking to Influence the Skeptical Listener

The power of persuasion ...

PERSUASIVE

Becoming Persuasive

Persuasion is the convincing of people to such a degree that they are compelled to ac. Leaders can only be successful as they move the people they influence to make decision and take actions.

Personal Insight: Persuasive

What does being persuasive mean to you? How does it relate to your current condition? In what ways will becoming more persuasive improve your situation?

_____

_____

_____

Altruism and Persuasive

Leaders persuade in sincere and holistic ways, always keeping the well-being and growth of those they persuade in mind. While an organizational goal may drive them, altruism, the fifth key characteristic of leadership, must be the bedrock of the persuasive activities. We seek the best solutions for all involved.

Heroic Altruism ⟩⟩⟩ Enthusiastic | Persuasive | Cooperative

Presentations and Persuasive

The persuasive presentation results in, well, results! Members of the audience, or the group as a whole, accept the presenter's opinion as worthwhile of action, and do.

PERSUASIVE

Training Objectives

Workshop objectives represent small goals designed to help us develop the leadership characteristic being deliberated. They provide both clear direction for our training activities, and a method for measuring successful application of the related content. They connect to the leadership skills we evaluated as part of our self-assessment at the start of our training.

As we diligently embrace these objectives, we will perceive positive changes in our performance and personality.

Persuasive Training Objectives	♥
1. Affirm our persuasive powers to stimulate positive change	
2. Analyze benefits and advantages to kindle a desire for action from listeners	
3. Weave stories into our entreaty to create urgency	

Linking to Presentations

Think back to the vision and mission for increasing dynamic presentations that we considered at the beginning of the training. Reflect on how this characteristic relates to our desire to become more dynamic.

=	How does becoming more persuasive support those aims? Why is increasing persuasion critical to becoming a successful leader?

> *Persuasion is often more effectual than force.*
> **—Aesop**

PERSUASIVE

Persuasive Powers

Persuasion is the practice of convincing people of something to such a degree that they are moved to take action. It has components of both emotional motivation and logical or intellectual decisiveness, similar to the psychology of consumerism. Among varying theories is the strong indication that we make emotional purchasing decisions justified with logic.

People resist being sold to, but tend to enjoy buying from producers. They are inspired by the emotions associated with consuming, but want to make the decision themselves for reasons that seem valid and defensible.

Reasons for Buying

There are potentially dozens of different reasons for being persuaded to accept a product or course of action. Some of the reasons are key.

- Pain avoidance
- Fear
- Pleasure seeking
- Genuine benefits

Analyze Direct Benefits

When our audience has a specific objective in mind or a problem to solve, the direct approach is typically the most persuasive. "We need to sell ten thousand widgets by the end of the year," they might say. "Here is a surefire method for selling ten thousand widgets this year," you respond, and the logical requisites are met.

Analyze Advantages

When evaluating the concepts being presented, objections may arise. If the presenter demonstrates a ready knowledge of potential criticisms or disadvantages, along with thoughtful solutions or responses, the persuasive characteristics are amplified.

- Keep the benefit descriptions simple
- Way to achieve existing goals
- Advantages to the call to action
- Potential disadvantages
- Analysis, comparison
- Confidently recommend best option

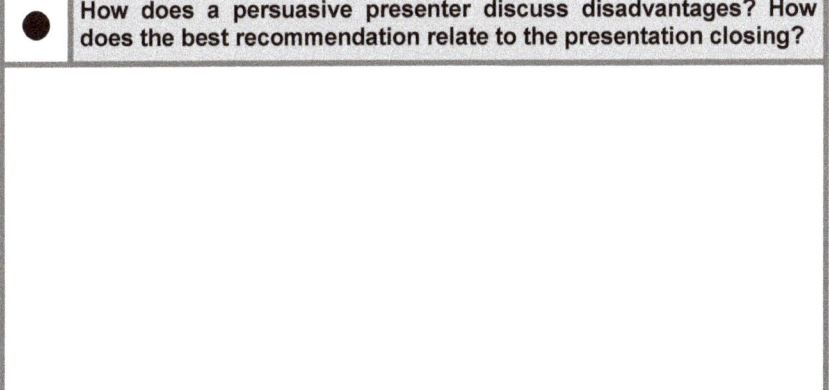

How does a persuasive presenter discuss disadvantages? How does the best recommendation relate to the presentation closing?

PERSUASIVE

Analyze Indirect Benefits

Along with the primary benefit used to persuade our audiences, secondary, indirect, or complimentary arguments might be needed to be most effective. When our listeners are skeptical or entrances, we can announce these types of indirect benefits to bring them to a decision.

> ➢ Do the right thing, right reasons
> ➢ Appeal to their self-concept
> ➢ Challenge them to new heights
> ➢ Benefit others through actions
> ➢ Join with others
> ➢ _____

■	**What is the danger of adding supplemental benefits to the call to action? What other persuaders might be utilized?**

> *Advertising is fundamentally persuasion and persuasion happens to be not a science, but an art.*
> —William Bernbach

PERSUASIVE

Weave Stories to Create Urgency

Our call to action, best recommendation, should have a suggested deadline in order to be most persuasive. Virtually all resources are scarce, especially that of time. Be sure to link the urgency of the concepts presented back to the maximization of benefits to remain consistent and genuine.

- Storytelling:
  - Humans relate through stories
  - Personal experiences
  - Second- and third-party
  - Historic
- Urgency of time
- Scarcity of supply
- _____

> **How can a good story create a sense of urgency?**

HEROIC ALTRUISM > DYNAMIC PRESENTATIONS > LEADERSHIP EXCELLENCE

PERSUASIVE

Practice Weaving Stories

Think of different stories you have heard about your operations at work. Consider tales of triumphs and woes, victories and sorrows from customer service, production, sales, finance, the corporate office, human resources, and the like. Which ones have you been involved with personally? Which ones are from another party? Do any predate your tenure at the company?

_____

_____

> ▲ Relate a story from your work experience and use it to create a sense of urgency. How natural was the process? How frequent are similar stories shared in your work environment?

Putting it All Together

Now is the time to put everything together. Review the objectives laid out at the beginning of this workshop, and the related principles we have discussed. Identify the topics that really hit home for you, those that will have an impact on future presentations. There may be subjects with which you are already comfortable when speaking to an audience, and others that might need a little more practice to make them powerful allies in developing your delivery skills. Incorporate them into this presentation.

Persuasive Presentation Instructions

Prepare a persuasive presentation to overcome a problem or seize an opportunity at work. Topics from professional settings are best. Include notes on how you will apply the principles reviewed in this workshop. Be sure to make use of all concepts we have reviewed to date.

- Topic: professional problem or opportunity
- Time Limit: 5 minutes
- Incorporate training objectives:
    - Analyze benefits
    - Weave stories to create urgency
    - Incorporate additional objectives

PERSUASIVE

Commitment: Persuasive Presentation

The quest for positive, exciting behavior change requires effort and stamina. It is for the strong-willed. In our workshop laboratory, we have explored activities contributing toward improved leadership. Continued practice and coaching will lead to mastery of the concepts and methods, ensuring solid, long-term results. Thank you for the authentic effort!

Prepare, Practice, and Report

Please prepare a Persuasive Presentation to practice outside of training and then report back to the lab participants. Consider your own development or the benefit of a co-worker when deciding who to involve.

I	Prepare details for your Persuasive Presentations commitment.

Presentation Title:

Open:

Analyze Benefits:

Suggested Solution:

Urgency through Storytelling:

Close:

Questions:

PERSUASIVE

Commitment Report Observations

As participants relate their commitment experiences, carefully watch their delivery. Note how they applied the principles we have discussed. Did they cover all aspects of the commitment? What specifically did they do well? Where were opportunities to coach for even more progress? What did you observe that you would like to appreciate, recognize, or adopt for yourself?

Observation Notes: Name, Compliment, Proof
1.
2.
3.
4.

Commitment Report Personal Debrief

Review the commitment report you just delivered. Consider your own input and feedback from the coach and fellow participants. List everything you did well, circling the one success that was most meaningful to you. Identify one challenge that will add the most leadership value to when improved.

All My Successes

_____

_____

_____

My One Greatest Challenge

_____

PERSUASIVE

Realized Benefits

We train to realize our vision, to develop tools to reach our goals, to become more excellent, and to assist others in doing the same. Having performed the related objectives, consider how they have moved us closer to attaining our vision and mission.

- ☑ Excellent
- ☐ Very good
- ☐ Good
- ☐ Average
- ☐ Poor

My Most Significant Benefit

Of all the benefits you may have experienced in this workshop, which one is the most significant for you, either professionally or personally? Why is this benefit essential to your leadership success?

_____

_____

_____

Benefitting Others

Our development serves to help those around us, our partners, teams, departments, and organizations. How will my most significant benefit impact those around me? Who in my circles of influence might also take advantage of this training to realize increased leadership success?

_____

_____

_____

_____

Additional Training

We all know that excellence does not happen by accident. It takes dedication, persistence, and wisdom to make lasting, positive improvements to our leadership skillsets. This training event is one of many designed to develop our full potential as leaders. What other topics might benefit you or your organization? Please speak with the coach about recommendations for pursuing these very topics in more depth, or alternate topics that are critical to your ongoing success.

PERSUASIVE

Persuasive Summary

Becoming persuasive culminates all past characteristics of a dynamic presenter. We learn how to not only relate our emotional commitment to our topic and present the information in a convincing manner, but we induce our audience to action. As we practice dynamic presentations, we become better leaders and impact the progress of others at the same time. We discussed three objectives:

1. Affirm persuasive powers
2. Analyze benefits and advantages
3. Weave stories to create urgency

There are a number of questions to contemplate as we summarize this workshop. What concepts will result in the most positive impact if applied regularly? Which ones should you put into action right away? Why are those key? Which principles will make the most difference for improved leadership in your work situation? How can I most benefit the team that I am responsible for leading? In which area do I need to improve the most?

> ■ **How does analyzing (dis)advantages increase persuasiveness in our presentations? When would avoiding it be more persuasive?**

> ■ **How can we make third-party and historic stories persuasive? In what situation would an historic story give a sense of urgency?**

PERSUASIVE

Persuasive Conclusion

If you would persuade, you must appeal to interest rather than intellect.
—Benjamin Franklin

Additional Notes

_____
_____
_____
_____
_____
_____
_____
_____
_____
_____
_____
_____
_____
_____
_____
_____

GUIDED PRESENTATIONS
Perfecting Our Craft with Directed Feedback

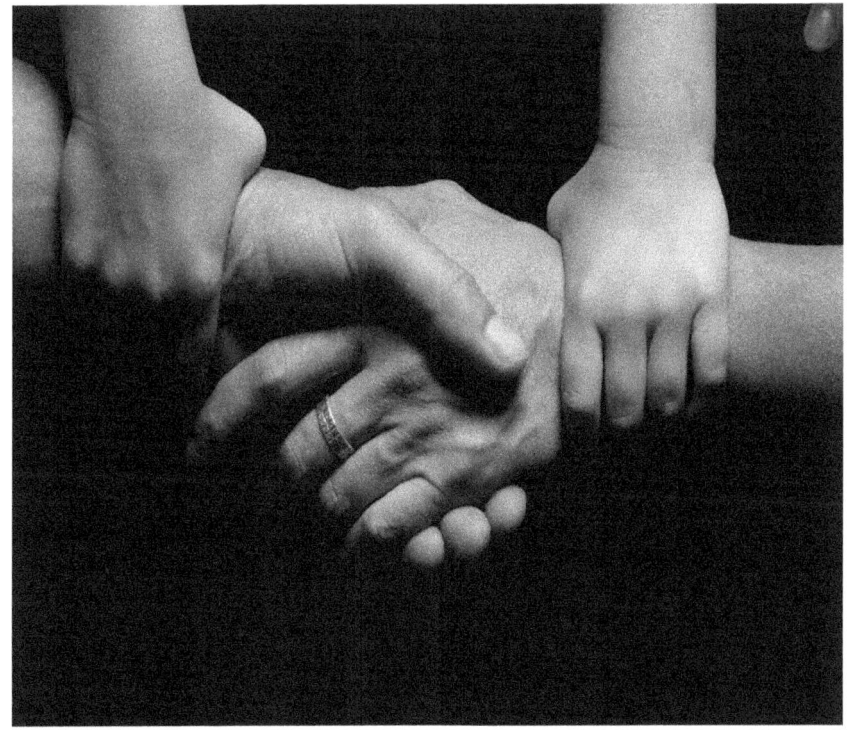

Climbing with a Sherpa ...

GUIDED

Becoming Guided

Guiding another person's progress requires both time and energy. When we guide others, or they guide us, an investment is made in the unique resource that maximizes an organization's ability to differentiate itself in the marketplace—its people!

Personal Insight: Guided

What does being guided mean to you? How does it relate to your current condition? In what ways will becoming more guided improve your situation?

_____

_____

_____

Coaching and Guided

Guiding a coworker is more than explaining what must be done. It involves taking that person by the hand and leading them towards their desired goal. It is a practical, serious approach to coaching.

Presentations and Guided

We become our best presenters as we receive guidance on how to overcome faults and improve strengths. The listening ear not only provides feedback, but returns again and again to witness improvement and keep its subjects on the path to achievement.

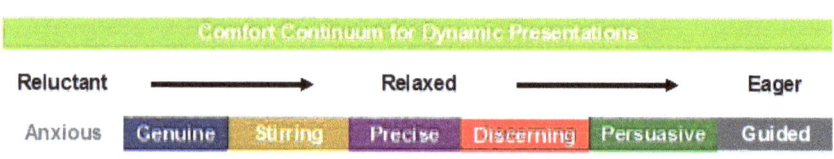

GUIDED

Training Objectives

Workshop objectives represent small goals designed to help us develop the leadership characteristic being deliberated. They provide both clear direction for our training activities, and a method for measuring successful application of the related content. They connect to the leadership skills we evaluated as part of our self-assessment at the start of our training.

As we diligently embrace these objectives, we will perceive positive changes in our performance and personality.

Guided Training Objectives	♥
1. Promote a determination to improve dynamic presentations	
2. Contribute to personal success through self-coaching	
3. Implement peer coaching to allow for continuous improvement	

Linking to Presentations

Think back to the vision and mission for increasing dynamic presentations that we considered at the beginning of the training. Reflect on how this characteristic relates to our desire to become more dynamic.

=	How does becoming more guided support those aims? Why is increasing guidance critical to becoming a successful leader?

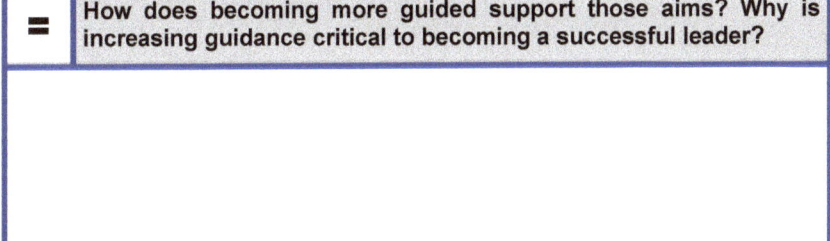

A coach is someone who tells you what you don't want to hear, who has you see what you don't want to see, so you can be who you always knew you could be.
—Tom Landry

Determination to Improve

As we move along the Comfort Continuum, we develop a sense of eagerness to speak to others, for our colleagues to digest and accept our ideas. This power of dynamic communication is a common trait among admired leaders. It builds on the engagement we have previously created, and provides confidence to become an effective team manager.

Reasons to Improve

Reasons for getting better vary widely, though engaged employees and powerful presenters tend to look inward and find personal motivation to continue the struggle that they know will reap coveted dividends.

- Extrinsic (tangible) rewards:
    - Bonuses, benefits, raises
    - Fame , recognition
    - Power, promotions, responsibility
    - Limited supply
- Intrinsic (abstract) rewards:
    - Personal satisfaction
    - Self-development
    - Success of organization
    - Unlimited supply

■ How can we better align impactful rewards with our current compensation systems? What will be the cost?

GUIDED

Success through Self-Coaching

Some situations will not allow for a traditional business coaching. It could be that your company has only a small number of employees, or that very few people are in a position to assist, or that the organizational culture is not supportive of coaching. Maybe we feel unduly sensitive to the coaching and are not quite ready ourselves.

We are always able to self-coach, to set goals for ourselves and plan practice session to work towards those goals.

- Follow leadership steps to set goals
- Attack the most critical skill first
- Self-coach as we would others
- Face yourself: realistic, mirror
- Report progress
- Seek a guide

 In what situations might we decided to guide ourselves towards our goals? When do we know we have reached the limit of our self-coaching effectiveness?

> *Encouraging companions, patient and true, give assurance to the mind and stamina to the heart.*
> —David Benson

The Choice Is Mine

We decide our future success or failure. We determine what we will achieve or not. When we decide to make the positive change, be the positive change we will see the start experiencing the improvement. The emotional change is difficult to conquer. Coaching is a boon to those wishing to become more excellent.

If you think you are beaten, you are
If you think you dare not, you don't,
If you like to win, but you think you can't
It is almost certain you won't.

If you think you'll lose, you're lost
For out of the world we find,
Success begins with a fellow's will
It's all in the state of mind.

If you think you are outclassed, you are
You've got to think high to rise,
You've got to be sure of yourself before
You can ever win a prize.

Life's battles don't always go
To the stronger or faster man,
But soon or late the man who wins
Is the man WHO THINKS HE CAN!

—Walter D. Wintle

GUIDED

Improvement through Peer Coaching

When we ask someone to help us improve, we make ourselves vulnerable emotionally, socially, and professionally. It can be a large risk! The core of coaching others is the honest desire to help them succeed. As we guide our colleagues and peers, we are reminded of the loyalty we owe them to be the true and faithful escorts they have entrusted us to be.

> - Sincerely attempt to add value
> - Always be positive
> - Focus on their objectives
> - Be flexible
> - Be discreet

> - _____

=	How can we discreetly guide our peers and still promote coaching in our organization? Why was the coach or colleague role more comfortable in this exercise?

CRUCIAL COACHING > DYNAMIC PRESENTATIONS > LEADERSHIP EXCELLENCE

GUIDED

Peer Coaching Criticism

When we are in earnest to help or be helped, we at times become vulnerable to hard feelings. We lash out in harshness, or receive kind words out of context and reject them in anger. It is easy to fall victim to the negativity of perceived unconstructive criticism. These situations are chances to demonstrate our dedication to coaching.

> Assume helpful motives
> Find value
> Accept *unjust* criticism with thanks
> Analyze mistakes, find deeper insights
> Rededicate to improvement

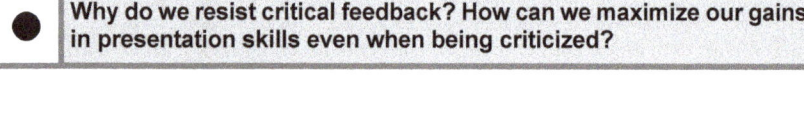

Why do we resist critical feedback? How can we maximize our gains in presentation skills even when being criticized?

Putting it All Together

Now is the time to put everything together. Review the objectives laid out at the beginning of this workshop, and the related principles we have discussed. Identify the topics that really hit home for you, those that will have an impact on future presentations. There may be subjects with which you are already comfortable when speaking to an audience, and others that might need a little more practice to make them powerful allies in developing your delivery skills. Incorporate them into this presentation.

Guided Presentation Instructions

Use the format of the Persuasive Presentation to guide a lab participant with a second peer coach. Take turns providing feedback and making course corrections to keep the presenter on track. Include feedback on how the presenter applies the principles reviewed in this and previous workshops.

- Topic: personal success story
- Time Limit: 5 minutes
- Incorporate training objectives:
    - Analyze benefits
    - Weave stories to create urgency
    - Incorporate additional objectives

GUIDED   David Benson Coaching

Commitment: Guided Presentation

The quest for positive, exciting behavior change requires effort and stamina. It is for the strong-willed. In our workshop laboratory, we have explored activities contributing toward improved leadership. Continued practice and coaching will lead to mastery of the concepts and methods, ensuring solid, long-term results. Thank you for the authentic effort!

Please prepare a Guided Presentation to practice during training in the laboratory with other lab participants. Consider the development of the person you are coaching.

!	Prepare details for your Guided Presentation commitment.

Presentation Title:

Open:

Analyze Benefits:

Suggested Solution:

Urgency through Storytelling:

Close:

Questions:

Commitment Report Observations

As participants relate their commitment experiences, carefully watch their delivery. Note how they applied the principles we have discussed. Did they cover all aspects of the commitment? What specifically did they do well? Where were opportunities to coach for even more progress? What did you observe that you would like to appreciate, recognize, or adopt for yourself?

Observation Notes: Name, Compliment, Proof
1.
2.
3.
4.

Commitment Report Personal Debrief

Review the commitment report you just delivered. Consider your own input and feedback from the coach and fellow participants. List everything you did well, circling the one success that was most meaningful to you. Identify one challenge that will add the most leadership value to when improved.

All My Successes

_____

_____

_____

My One Greatest Challenge

_____

GUIDED   David Benson Coaching

Realized Benefits

We train to realize our vision, to develop tools to reach our goals, to become more excellent, and to assist others in doing the same. Having performed the related objectives, consider how they have moved us closer to attaining our vision and mission.

☑ Excellent
☐ Very good
☐ Good
☐ Average
☐ Poor

My Most Significant Benefit

Of all the benefits you may have experienced in this workshop, which one is the most significant for you, either professionally or personally? Why is this benefit essential to your leadership success?

_____

_____

_____

Benefitting Others

Our development serves to help those around us, our partners, teams, departments, and organizations. How will my most significant benefit impact those around me? Who in my circles of influence might also take advantage of this training to realize increased leadership success?

_____

_____

_____

_____

Executive Coaching

Determined to supercharge culture and obliterate obstacles? Enlist our coaching services to make a lasting impact for your organization. Participants are held accountable for developing the improved skills and new habits they desire, with guided follow-up to ensure success. Executive coaching is also available for individuals ready to take their leadership game to the next level. Please speak with the coach if about executive coaching for your members of your organization.

Guided Summary

We guide people to improve because we house an earnest desire to see them reach their goals. As we coach them and ourselves, taking advantage of criticism, we smooth our rough presentation edges until our influence is pronounced. As we practice dynamic presentations, we become better leaders and impact the progress of others at the same time. We discussed three objectives:

1. Promote a determination to improve
2. Succeed through self-coaching
3. Improve through peer coaching

There are a number of questions to contemplate as we summarize this workshop. What concepts will result in the most positive impact if applied regularly? Which ones should you put into action right away? Why are those key? Which principles will make the most difference for improved leadership in your work situation? How can I most benefit the team that I am responsible for leading? In which area do I need to improve the most?

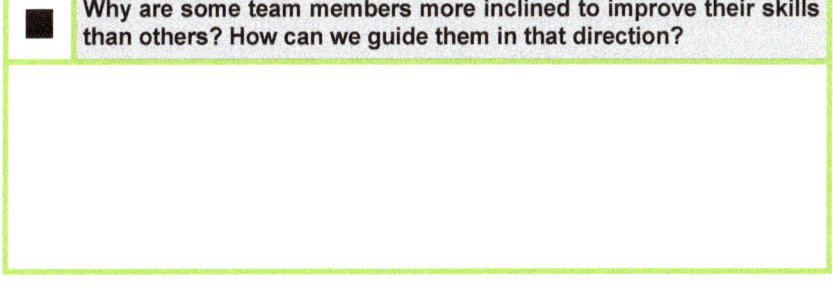

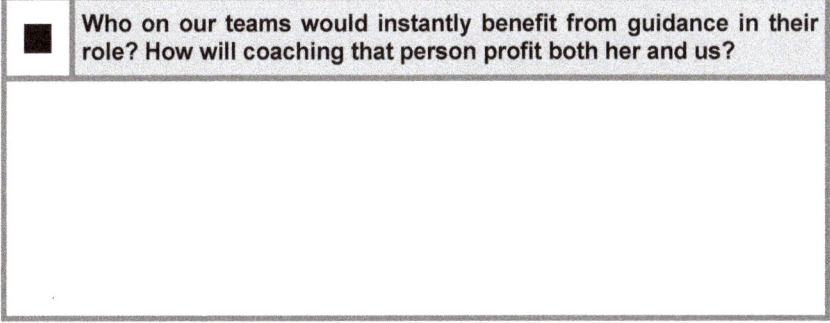

GUIDED

Guided Conclusion

> *What makes a good coach?*
> *Complete dedication.*
>
> —George Halas

Additional Notes

_____
_____
_____
_____
_____
_____
_____
_____
_____
_____
_____
_____
_____
_____
_____
_____

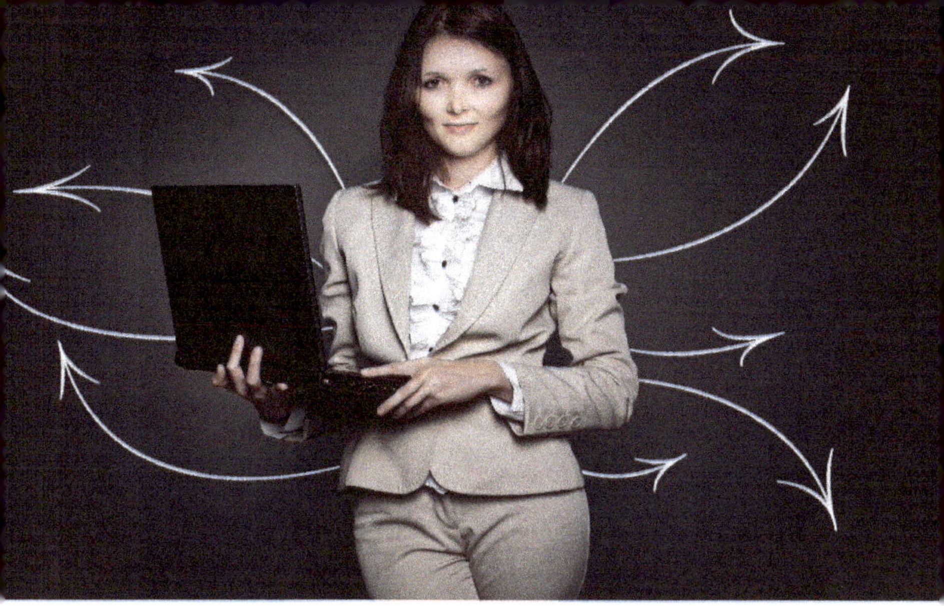

EFFECTIVE MANAGEMENT TRACK
Guiding Competent Teams

_____
Participant Name

MANAGEMENT

Leadership and Management

We have heard that the only constant in the universe is change, and the professional development world is no different. It seems new research is regularly leading to new models, techniques, and fads. Learners pursuing leadership excellence need only focus on enduring principles to succeed, aiming at clear, written, vibrant targets to measure progress.

 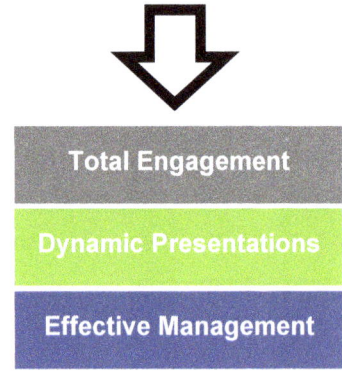

Developing the skills to lead people in management roles takes effort, courage, and risk. Whether looking to manage small teams, large departments or divisions, or entire organizations, we become esteemed as we increase our effectiveness. Progression along the esteem continuum starts with being candid, then resolute, refined, vigorous, cooperative, and finally mentored.

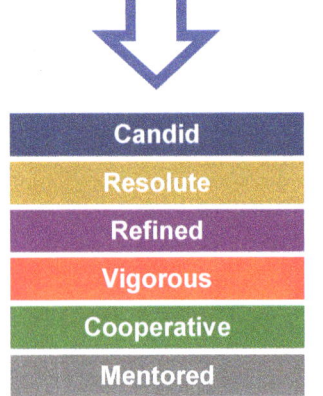

As part of the Leadership Excellence course, this two-day Effective Management track will address how those with authority should apply the six leadership characteristics to best lead the people they supervise.

A manager's esteem from colleagues climaxes as they become cooperative and are mentored by a concerned advisor. It is only then that their full worth as a leader is realized, and they approach fulfillment of their potential in their chosen domain.

MANAGEMENT

Introducing Management

Management as the capable influencing, manipulation, and organizing, and marshalling of systems and people is a key aspect of leadership. It is the coordination of organizational activities to achieve certain objectives or goals, and in this respect is closely tied to organizational leadership. Management is in many respects where the rubber hits the road, with practical application of business principles. Excellent leaders must be effective managers.

Quotations

Schools of business and management libraries are full of literary works discussing how management differs from leadership. Both are necessary, and the more effective a manager one becomes, the more excellent a leader she may be.

> *A leader is the one who can outline the broad vision and the direction, and say here's where we are going to go, here's why we need to go there, and here's how we are going to get there. A manager is the one who actually gets up under the hood and tunes the carburetor.*
> —Mike Huckabee

> *Good management is the art of making problems so interesting and their solutions so constructive that everyone wants to get to work and deal with them.*
> —Paul Hawken

MANAGEMENT

Management Self-Assessment

Please frankly assess yourself for each leadership skill below based on your current situation using a scale from 0-10 (*never* to *always*). Rate your abilities before training, then again after the training is complete.

Leadership Skills to Measure	Before	After	+ / -
1. I remain open to personal feedback from others.			
2. I hold myself and my team accountable.			
3. My rewards tend to be intangible or internal.			
4. My staff has a unified vision for our work.			
5. Every member of my team provides input to our decisions.			
6. I use team goals as effective tools.			
7. My team routinely makes great stride forward.			
8. I effectively help my staff correct mistakes.			
9. I listen honestly, clearly, and with empathy.			
10. Our staff meetings are productive and useful.			
11. I regularly invest time and effort into my people.			
12. I delegate responsibilities to develop my staff.			
Assessment Totals (120 points max.)			

Once the management training has ended and the above assessment complete, please identify the most significant value, benefit, or gain for:

13. You as an individual, professionally, personally, or otherwise.

_____

_____

14. Your organization, business, community, or other relationships.

_____

_____

Personality Change

The phrase *you are what you eat* may be true to some degree, but the more important realization is that we are what we experience. We are what we think, feel, express, and do. Our personality is the intricate blend of our emotional and behavioral characteristics or traits that uniquely distinguish us from each other. We form our personality by our thoughts and actions.

Improvement only occurs when we make a decision to shift our emotions and behavior in some direction. Changing either without the other is insufficient, and though excellence can be difficult, it can be achieved when we work towards it.

$$PC = EC \times IC \times BC$$

Transforming Management

Think of the many possible benefits you might realize through this effective management training. What do you want to improve about yourself as an individual or a leader? How about in your teams, or in your work situation generally? What admirable qualities, habits, or processes do you see elsewhere that you would like to adopt for yourself? What would you need to get out of this training to make it completely and utterly worthwhile?

_____

_____

_____

_____

_____

_____

_____

MANAGEMENT

Becoming Effective

Managing people and projects, leading them to realize visions and goals, can be the most challenging and rewarding activities in our professional lives. While management can exist without leading, leadership demands management. As we become more effective at managing our people and tasks, we grow into an improved leader.

Identity

We wear many hats in many divergent situations. For the purposes of this training, determine your primary title, position, or role in your organization.

I	**Please record <u>who</u> you are for our training purposes.**

Vision

An inspiring statement of purpose or motivation describes our future, ideal situation. Briefly state your vision of a more effective leader.

●	**Please record <u>why</u> you want to increase team effectiveness.**

Mission

A single, ambitious, overarching goal defines what we will do to realize our vision. This has more detail, covering all aspects of our work. Subordinate milestones and tasks support it. Briefly state your management mission.

↱	**Please record <u>what</u> you will do to achieve your management vision.**

CANDID MANAGEMENT
Pledging Frankness in Our Work

I always feels like somebody's watching me ...

CANDID

David Benson Coaching

Becoming Candid

When we are candid, we are not just truthful, but we are also forthright and frank about the truth. We temper our discourse so that we are not overly blunt, but we are equally bold in explaining things as we see them. Like a candid photo, we naturally portray who we really are, without pretense.

Personal Insight: Candid

What does being candid mean to you? How does it relate to our opening activity/discussion? In what ways will becoming more candid improve your current situation?

_____

_____

_____

Integrity and Candid

Becoming more candid culminates our journey towards increased integrity, the first key characteristic of leadership. Our personal confidence allows us to be more genuine, which in turn gives us the courage to be plainspoken and direct with regard to the activities of others, and our team situation.

| Intrepid Integrity | >>> | Confident | Genuine | Candid |

Management and Candid

The people we lead appreciate hearing the truth unvarnished and without caveats. Even difficult news is best shared with those with whom we work in an upfront manner, for they understand that we trust ourselves and them enough to be open with all relevant aspects of the situation. Their esteem for us increases as they know we will not unduly shelter them from either the circumstances, or their own decisions.

Training Objectives

Workshop objectives represent small goals designed to help us develop the leadership characteristic being deliberated. They provide both clear direction for our training activities, and a method for measuring successful application of the related content. They connect to the leadership skills we evaluated as part of our self-assessment at the start of our training.

As we diligently embrace these objectives, we will perceive positive changes in our performance and personality.

Candid Training Objectives	♥
1. Appreciate the significance of leading by example	
2. Uncover blind spots in our leadership	
3. Establish accountability for job descriptions and duties among our personnel	

Linking to Management

Think back to the vision and mission for increasing effective management that we considered at the beginning of the training. Reflect on how this characteristic relates to our desire to become more effective.

=	How does becoming more candid support those aims? Why is increasing effectiveness critical to becoming a successful leader?

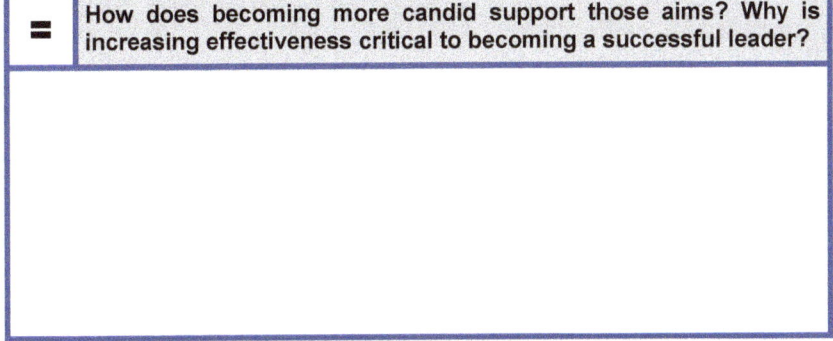

Your actions speak so loudly, I cannot hear what you are saying.
—Ralph Waldo Emerson

CANDID   David Benson Coaching

Lead by Example

The people for whom we are responsible need to know that we are willing, and often able, to do the tasks we require of them. We lead from the front of the team, not from the rear. Consider the quotation on the previous page. How does the concept correspond to excellent leadership?

_____

_____

Ways to Lead by Example

It is unreasonable for a leader to perform every task her subordinates must do every day. How, then are we able to lead by example?

- ➤ Relate past experiences
- ➤ Demonstrate how to perform a task
- ➤ Respond to questions
- ➤ Cover for absent team members
- ➤ Assist with undesirable activities

▲	What other methods are there to lead by example? In what way does your current supervisor earn your trust in leading by example?

Walk the Talk

As we lead our team members by practicing what we preach, we should be aware of those who may need extra guidance. Not everyone is able to keep pace with our example, and we should be candid about helping them catch up with our stride, whether it be individual our in a team environment.

> ➢ Provide context: who, why, what
> ➢ Slow it down
> ➢ Chunk it up
> ➢ Repeat it often

EDGE for Success

The Boy Scouts of America have developed a leadership tool for helping their members teach different skills. They call it the EDGE Method: explain, demonstrate, guide, and enable.

CANDID   David Benson Coaching

Uncover Blind Spots

We know a lot about ourselves, but there are some aspects of our behavior or personality that remain hidden to us. Even the mirror, introspection, can only reveal what we allow it to show. We need those around us to provide a more complete, clear, candid picture of who we are.

Johari Window

The Johari Window reveals how other people can show us things about ourselves that we may never have seen.

	YOU Known	YOU Unknown
OTHERS Known	ARENA (Public, Open)	BLIND SPOT
OTHERS Unknown	FACADE (Avoided, Hidden)	UNKNOWN

> = What can your lab partner reveal about your personality that you may not already comprehend? Get help discovering her feedback.

Leading the Blind

By definition we cannot be aware of those aspects of our character that we do not notice. It is like being asked to describe the furnishings of a room while wearing a blindfold. We have not seen the room, so how can we possibly describe its contents? And yet, becoming the excellent leader we envision requires us making changes for the better.

Willing Assistants

We are surrounded by people who know things about us that we are currently unable to perceive. Some are well-known, while others may seem unlikely assistants.

> **=** **List as many different types of associates who might assist with our blindness. How did working with your partner help?**

Reasons to Assist

With so many people who could help us better understand ourselves, only a subset actually would. Consider why some of our associates might be more willing to assist than others.

> **=** **What leadership techniques have we discussed that might encourage our associates to help us out?**

CANDID

Plainly Define Responsibilities

Clearly understanding who we are, where we fit in the organization, and how we contribute are key to business integrity. As a leader, it is vital that we communicate these responsibilities to our team members so that we can be the most effective.

Affinity Diagram for Job Description

An affinity diagram is a useful tool for analyzing our primary work responsibilities. Columns represent major performance areas, and details within columns describe regular tasks and activities.

> ● Did you uncover any blind spots? Are there responsibilities that can be shifted to another role? What is missing from your description?

Establish Accountability

We are responsible for our own thoughts, actions, biases, successes, and failures. We are also accountable for the actions of groups or systems under our control. As leaders, we must hold ourselves and others accountable for achieving the goals we have set.

Management Time: Who's Got the Monkey?

The above article was first published in Harvard Business Review in 1974, by William Oncken, Jr. and Donald L. Wass.

- Boss-imposed time
- Self-imposed time (discretionary)
- System-imposed time (peers)
- Subordinate-imposed time (also…?)

> For which types of time or activities are we accountable? What *monkeys* do we often pass back and forth?

> *It is true that integrity alone won't make you a leader, but without integrity you will never be one.*
> —Zig Ziglar

CANDID   David Benson Coaching

Commitment: Candid Management

The quest for positive, exciting behavior change requires effort and stamina. It is for the strong-willed. In our workshop laboratory, we have explored activities contributing toward improved leadership. Continued practice and coaching will lead to mastery of the concepts and methods, ensuring solid, long-term results. Thank you for the authentic effort!

Prepare, Practice, and Report

Please prepare a Candid Management activity to practice outside of training and then report back to the lab participants. Consider your own development or the benefit of a co-worker when deciding who to involve.

I	Prepare details for your Candid Management commitment.

Candid Management Task:

Who to Involve:

Why This Is Important:

What I Will Do:

How I Will Do It:

Commitment Report Observations

As participants relate their commitment experiences, carefully watch their delivery. Note how they applied the principles we have discussed. Did they cover all aspects of the commitment? What specifically did they do well? Where were opportunities to coach for even more progress? What did you observe that you would like to appreciate, recognize, or adopt for yourself?

Observation Notes: Name, Compliment, Proof
1.
2.
3.
4.

Commitment Report Personal Debrief

Review the commitment report you just delivered. Consider your own input and feedback from the coach and fellow participants. List everything you did well, circling the one success that was most meaningful to you. Identify one challenge that will add the most leadership value to when improved.

All My Successes

_____

_____

_____

My One Greatest Challenge

_____

CANDID

David Benson Coaching

Realized Benefits

We train to realize our vision, to develop tools to reach our goals, to become more excellent, and to assist others in doing the same. Having performed the related objectives, consider how they have moved us closer to attaining our vision and mission.

☑ Excellent
☐ Very good
☐ Good
☐ Average
☐ Poor

My Most Significant Benefit

Of all the benefits you may have experienced in this workshop, which one is the most significant for you, either professionally or personally? Why is this benefit essential to your leadership success?

_____

_____

_____

Benefitting Others

Our development serves to help those around us, our partners, teams, departments, and organizations. How will my most significant benefit impact those around me? Who in my circles of influence might also take advantage of this training to realize increased leadership success?

_____

_____

_____

_____

Helping Others Succeed

When we have a personal or professional breakthrough, we instinctively look to share the benefit with those close to us. We want them to succeed as well. Think of team members, colleagues, industry friends, even local neighbors who are seeking to improve their current situation, to become more excellent leaders. Who among them would be responsive to leadership training? Please speak with the coach about how to involve them in this very same or subsequent training events.

Candid Summary

On our journey towards increased candor as a part of management effectiveness, we have considered three objectives concepts relating to becoming more candid. We discussed three objectives:

1. Appreciate leading by example
2. Uncover blind spots in our leadership
3. Establish accountability among personnel

There are a number of questions to contemplate as we summarize this workshop. What concepts will result in the most positive impact if applied regularly? Which ones should be put into action right away? Why are those key? Which principles will make the most difference for improved leadership in your work situation? How can I most benefit the team that I am responsible for leading? In which area do I need to improve the most?

How will speaking candidly impact your team members?

Pinpoint a specific situation where these techniques can be used right away. Why that situation?

CANDID

Candid Conclusion

When you point the finger, you miss the point.
—Bruce D. Schneider

Additional Notes

_____
_____
_____
_____
_____
_____
_____
_____
_____
_____
_____
_____
_____
_____
_____
_____

RESOLUTE MANAGEMENT
Discovering Tenacity to Advance Our Cause

Hang in there, baby …

RESOLUTE

Becoming Resolute

When we are resolute, we are unwavering in our determination. Nothing will prevent us from our purpose, and nobody is able to dissuade us from our goals. We have reached the point when doubt and fear fade to the background, leaving only our future image.

Personal Insight: Resolute

What does being resolute mean to you? How does it relate to your current condition? In what ways will becoming more resolute improve your situation?

_____

_____

_____

Motivation and Resolute

Becoming resolute solidifies our motivation, the second key characteristic of leadership. While it still needs to be refreshed and remembered, the strength of our drive is now without parallel. At this point, only we can change the direction of our activities.

Management and Resolute

With an end result firmly fixed in our own minds, we are able to convey that same conviction to those we lead. Our teams become more determined along with us, and our ability to complete tasks and achieve goals efficiently becomes unmatched. We grow closer to becoming a respected leader.

Esteem Continuum for Effective Management						
Recognized	→		Respected	→		Admired
Ineffective	Candid	Resolute	Refined	Vigorous	Cooperative	Mentored

Training Objectives

Workshop objectives represent small goals designed to help us develop the leadership characteristic being deliberated. They provide both clear direction for our training activities, and a method for measuring successful application of the related content. They connect to the leadership skills we evaluated as part of our self-assessment at the start of our training.

As we diligently embrace these objectives, we will perceive positive changes in our performance and personality.

Resolute Training Objectives	♥
1. Produce internal motivation to realize a determined workforce	
2. Make the work its own reward to expand office cheerfulness	
3. Unite staff in vision to foster a cohesive team	

Linking to Management

Think back to the vision and mission for increasing effective management that we considered at the beginning of the training. Reflect on how this characteristic relates to our desire to become more effective.

=	How does becoming more resolute support those aims? Why is increasing resoluteness critical to becoming a successful leader?

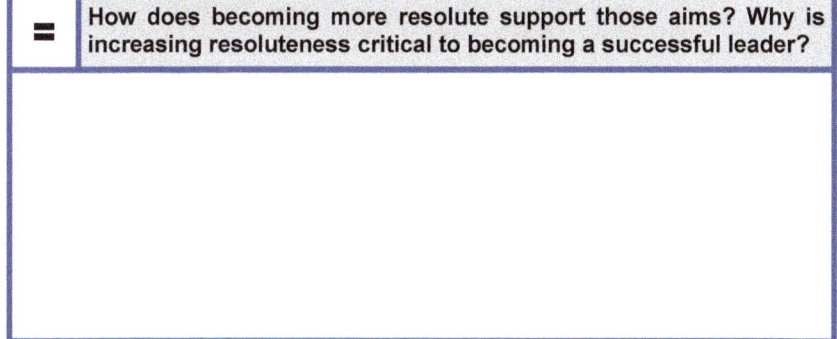

The truest wisdom is a resolute determination.
—Napoleon Bonaparte

Internal Motivation

Motivation is generally classified as either internal or external to the person or entity being motivated. When we think of internal motivation, we consider that it is not physical, but thoughts, feelings, or beliefs that push us toward a goal, the intangibles that really make the motivational change.

Hierarchy of Needs

Abraham Maslow first published his theory on motivation in 1943. Once the basic, lower-level needs are met, people focus on the higher-level needs. Before his death in 1970, he had added three additional levels: cognitive, aesthetic, and transcendence.

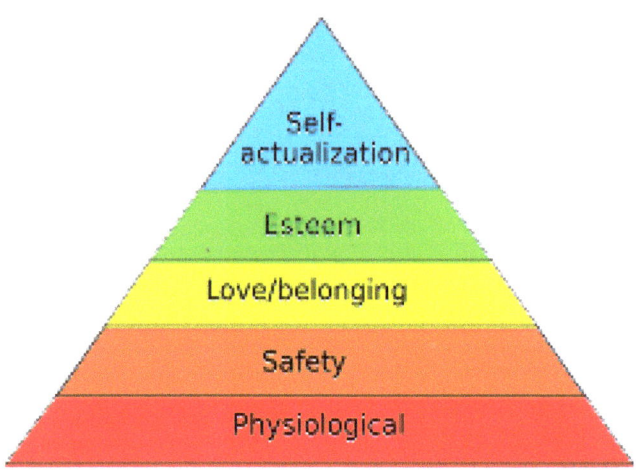

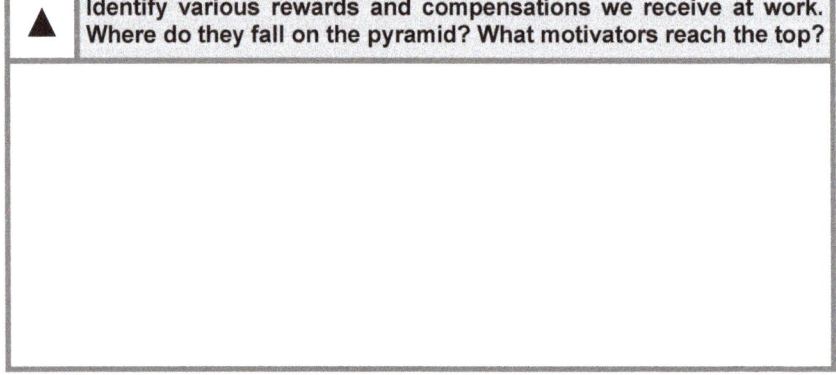

▲ Identify various rewards and compensations we receive at work. Where do they fall on the pyramid? What motivators reach the top?

RESOLUTE

Unshakeable Resolve

How does our resolve become unshakeable? Why is approximating this condition important to our success? What are the downsides?

_____

_____

_____

Driven to Succeed

Some people are famous for unwavering determination, even in the face of outrageous obstacles. Perhaps we admire them more because of their obstacles.

- Winston Churchill
- Florence Chadwick
- Thomas Edison
- Michael Jordan
- _____

> ▲ **Which example is most motivating to you? Why? What kept these legends moving forward when times were difficult?**

RESOLUTE   David Benson Coaching

Its Own Reward

We may have encountered expressions of joy related to work.

I cannot believe I get paid to do this work. I would do this whether I was paid or not.
—David Benson

Find a job you enjoy doing, and you will never have to work a day in your life.
—Mark Twain

Meaningful Work

When our group members fail to see the meaning in our work, it is up to the leaders to help them form a firm resolve. Becoming connected to the benefactor of our goods and services fosters this resolve.

- ➢ Hear from customers
- ➢ Meet the customers
- ➢ Become the customer: real or theoretical

■	**How can we get our staff more involved with our customers? How would this help staff motivation?**

REAL MOTIVATION > EFFECTIVE MANAGEMENT > LEADERSHIP EXCELLENCE

Vision Statement Defined

In addition to our values, our vision of an ideal future, a time of success and prosperity and happiness, motivates us to set goals and take action to realize it. Like a hoped-for dream, we see in our mind's eye all the beautiful possibilities, and yearn to experience them. They are typically based on values that are shared within an organization, and like values, change only on occasion.

A vision statement is designed to inspire. Its brief yet poignant message sweeps aside innocuous details and presents a powerful, sometimes archetypal image, tinged with emotion. When individual drivers match a group vision, the shared synergy can be dramatic. The primary elements of a vision are listed below.

- View of our ideal situation, the *dream*
- Inspiring, passionate, emotive
- Lengthy duration (entity lifetime?)
- No reference to specifics

Vision Examples

Here are some sample vision statements from renowned companies.

- Charles Schwab: Helping investors help themselves.
- Cold Stone Creamery: The ultimate ice cream experience
- Instagram: Capture and share the world of moments.
- Walt Disney: To make people happy.

Personal Vision Statement

A clear vision can provide stamina for demanding times and overwhelming situations, and the more daring or bold the vision, the more resilient to a grim present it can be. The statements on the previous page are certainly ambitious, easy to remember, and simple to communicate among managers, employees, customers, and the general public.

> **I** Referencing your earlier leadership vision notes, create a personal vision statement for your current position within your organization.

Vision Story

A vision story has the same motivational purpose as a statement, but affords more space to paint a powerful picture. Colorful images and optimistic language form vivid, larger-than-life depictions of that idealistic future as if it already existed, and we are simply describing it from the future, like a reporter excited to be a part of something wonderful.

> **=** Expound on your personal vision statement and create an in-depth vision story: present, powerful, and positive.

United in Vision

Engaged employees and volunteers typically share values with the organizations to which they belong. These values form the basis for a shared vision as well. This relatedness binds the individual to the group, and promotes a communal purpose. Meanwhile, there may be many layers to the organization, each with distinct versions or flavors of the overall values and vision

- Organization
- Division, department
- Team
- Individual

Coordinated Vision

Forming a team vision, somewhere between the organization and the individuals, unties our small groups to accomplish their goals.

 Create a team or small group vision that combines the overall organizational vision with those of the team members.

> *The truest wisdom is a resolute determination.*
> —Napoleon Bonaparte

RESOLUTE   David Benson Coaching

Commitment: Resolute Management

The quest for positive, exciting behavior change requires effort and stamina. It is for the strong-willed. In our workshop laboratory, we have explored activities contributing toward improved leadership. Continued practice and coaching will lead to mastery of the concepts and methods, ensuring solid, long-term results. Thank you for the authentic effort!

Prepare, Practice, and Report

Please prepare a Resolute Management activity to practice outside of training and then report back to the lab participants. Consider your own development or the benefit of a co-worker when deciding who to involve.

I — Prepare details for your Resolute Management commitment.

Resolute Management Task:

Who to Involve:

Why This Is Important:

What I Will Do:

How I Will Do It:

REAL MOTIVATION > EFFECTIVE MANAGEMENT > LEADERSHIP EXCELLENCE

Commitment Report Observations

As participants relate their commitment experiences, carefully watch their delivery. Note how they applied the principles we have discussed. Did they cover all aspects of the commitment? What specifically did they do well? Where were opportunities to coach for even more progress? What did you observe that you would like to appreciate, recognize, or adopt for yourself?

Observation Notes: Name, Compliment, Proof
1.
2.
3.
4.

Commitment Report Personal Debrief

Review the commitment report you just delivered. Consider your own input and feedback from the coach and fellow participants. List everything you did well, circling the one success that was most meaningful to you. Identify one challenge that will add the most leadership value to when improved.

All My Successes

_____

_____

_____

My One Greatest Challenge

_____

REAL MOTIVATION > EFFECTIVE MANAGEMENT > LEADERSHIP EXCELLENCE

Realized Benefits

We train to realize our vision, to develop tools to reach our goals, to become more excellent, and to assist others in doing the same. Having performed the related objectives, consider how they have moved us closer to attaining our vision and mission.

☑ Excellent
☐ Very good
☐ Good
☐ Average
☐ Poor

My Most Significant Benefit
Of all the benefits you may have experienced in this workshop, which one is the most significant for you, either professionally or personally? Why is this benefit essential to your leadership success?

_____

_____

_____

Benefitting Others
Our development serves to help those around us, our partners, teams, departments, and organizations. How will my most significant benefit impact those around me? Who in my circles of influence might also take advantage of this training to realize increased leadership success?

_____

_____

_____

_____

Motivational Speaking

Motivational? Of course! But our speaking engagements deliver so much more than the quickly fading warm fuzzy. Allow us to provide practical exercises and uplifting coaching as your keynote, break-out, or workshop speaker. Select from one of our many leadership excellence topics, or provide a custom subject to match your conference, convocation, or corporate retreat theme. Please speak with the coach about upcoming speaking opportunities for your organization.

RESOLUTE

Resolute Summary

On our journey towards increased motivation and management effectiveness, we have considered several concepts relating to becoming more resolute. We discussed three objectives:

1. Produce internal motivation
2. Make the work its own reward
3. Unite staff in vision

There are a number of questions to contemplate as we summarize this workshop. What concepts will result in the most positive impact if applied regularly? Which ones should you put into action right away? Why are those key? Which principles will make the most difference for improved leadership in your work situation? How can I most benefit the team that I am responsible for leading? In which area do I need to improve the most?

■ **Identify situations at work where external rewards can be replaced with internal rewards. How might that affect motivation?**

■ **Why will uniting our teams in shared values and vision lead to accomplishing our shared goals?**

RESOLUTE

Resolute Conclusion

The greatest day in your life and mine is when we take total responsibility for our attitudes. That's the day we truly grow up.

—John Maxwell

Additional Notes

REFINED MANAGEMENT
Taming Priorities from Competing Demands

Frankly, my dear, I don't give a straw ...

REFINED

Becoming Refined

With intense heat, a refiner's fire removes impurities until only the desired material remains. When our mission is pure with regard to our vision, nothing remains to get in our way or distract us from the success we desire.

Personal Insight: Refined

What does being refined mean to you? How does it relate to your current condition? In what ways will becoming more refined improve your situation?

_____

_____

_____

Strategy and Refined

When establishing our strategy, the third leadership characteristic, we will need to remove any superfluous or extra goals that do not align with the original intent. We will also need to adjust our plans to ensure they are taking us down the path that we wish.

Sound Strategy ➤➤➤ **Endorsed** | **Precise** | **Refined**

Management and Refined

As we update and perfect our plans, we gain an advantage as we employ the input and skill of our team members. As we have discussed, they see things we cannot – faults, obstacles, problems – and can help move through or around those issues. Our esteem grows as we welcome others to share in our vision, and ask for their assistance in achieving it.

REFINED

Training Objectives

Workshop objectives represent small goals designed to help us develop the leadership characteristic being deliberated. They provide both clear direction for our training activities, and a method for measuring successful application of the related content. They connect to the leadership skills we evaluated as part of our self-assessment at the start of our training.

As we diligently embrace these objectives, we will perceive positive changes in our performance and personality.

	Refined Training Objectives	♥
1.	Align mission statements to prepare for future success	
2.	Welcome input from colleagues to discover hidden opportunities	
3.	Create goals to achieve better gains through focused efforts	

Linking to Management

Think back to the vision and mission for increasing effective management that we considered at the beginning of the training. Reflect on how this characteristic relates to our desire to become more effective.

=	How does becoming more refined support those aims? Why is increasing refinement critical to becoming a successful leader?

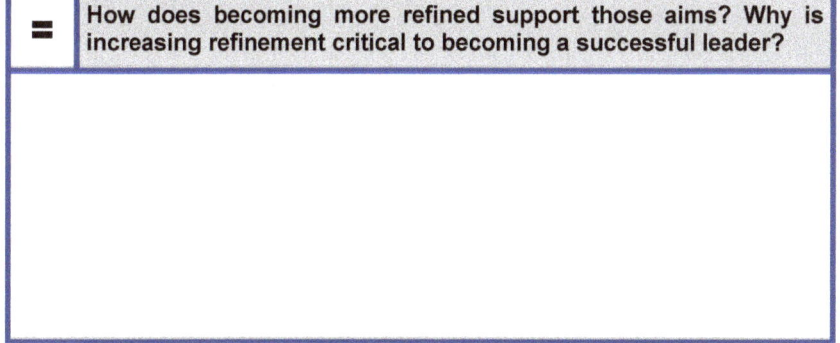

The key is not to prioritize what's on your schedule, but to schedule your priorities.
—Stephen Covey

SOUND STRATEGY > EFFECTIVE MANAGEMENT > LEADERSHIP EXCELLENCE

REFINED

Mission Statement Defined

Once our people are comfortable sharing their opinions with use, we are able to take full advantage of their intelligence, insights, and wisdom to set goals. Two heads are better than one, and if our group goals are ambitious, we will want as many heads as possible on our side.

The most important of these goals, the mission statement, is an expression of what we need to do to realize our vision. It is the starting point from which all other goals sprout. Our team members should provide their opinions for their personal, positional missions. Aspects of the mission statement are more generalized than subordinate goals, which have greater detail. Key elements include the following.

- What we do
- For whom we do it
- How we do it: best, fast, low-cost
- More lengthy than vision statement
- Indeterminate duration
- Subjective measurement

Mission Statement Example

Thousands of businesses and individuals have created mission statements to help guide their activities. The 2013 Walt Disney mission is a good example. Does it include all the key elements?

The Walt Disney Company's objective is to be one of the world's leading producers and providers of entertainment and information, using its portfolio of brands to differentiate its content, services and consumer products. The company's primary financial goals are to maximize earnings and cash flow, and to allocate capital toward growth initiatives that will drive long-term shareholder value.

SOUND STRATEGY > EFFECTIVE MANAGEMENT > LEADERSHIP EXCELLENCE

REFINED

Personal Mission Statement

Refer to your earlier leadership mission notes to gather some ideas about a mission statement for your role at your organization. How will you achieve your stated leadership vision? Create a positional mission statement for your current business title. How will a similar statement for your subordinates encourage engagement?

	Create a personal mission statement based on your current work position. What will be the impact on your effectiveness?

Mission Cards

The human subconscious is a powerful tool that we can tap to help achieve our mission. Mission cards are note cards covered in colorful, evocative images that we prominently place where we will constantly see them. The regular visual reminder of our mission, subordinate goals, or major tasks helps us keep focus, but also employs our subconscious to find solutions.

	Create a mission card to represent your statement. Will it work?

REFINED

United in Mission

The overall mission sets the tone and pace for all of our subordinate goals. In this track, we have set an initial goal for our management effectiveness. That should lead to other goals within our areas of responsibility that support the overall mission. The scope of a mission statement can vary from corporate, to team, to personal.

Team Mission Statement

We can make our mission statement a practical starting point with a few adjustments.

- Ensure a lengthy term (indefinite?)
- Appropriate scope
- Covers all responsibilities
- Audacious

▲ Create a division, department, or team mission statement to achieve the related vision. Is the mission motivating like the vision?

REFINED

Welcome Input

When we involve others in making our mission plans, we benefit in two related ways: 1) we gain insights that only our unique team members can bring to the table, and 2) we build up those team members so that they have a desire to continue contributing. Perhaps the largest benefit is that the contributors are determined to achieve those goals because they created them.

Green Light Thinking

When the green light is on, all ideas are welcome. There are truly no *bad* ideas in such a brain-storming session, and all judgement is left outside the room. The ideas should flow freely.

- Invite everyone to participate
- Explain the purpose
- Set a time limit
- Refrain from ANY judgement
- Quantity over quality

> **Why might we instigate a green-light session at work? How do we ensure everyone is heard? Does this even matter?**

SOUND STRATEGY > EFFECTIVE MANAGEMENT > LEADERSHIP EXCELLENCE

REFINED

David Benson Coaching

Plan for Opportunities

Planning for success should be a significant percentage of our work, some say as much as $25 to 40% of a project. This is because it is much easier to achieve a destination by following a complete, detailed, aligned roadmap than to start off blindly. Once we know our route, the planning aspect of the trip takes much less effort.

Planning Process

There are many acceptable models for the planning process, which may vary from one industry or objective to another. The most important aspects of the process are: 1) make a plan, and 2) follow the plan.

> ➢ Identify problem or challenge
> ➢ Green-light to gather ideas
> ➢ Red-light to determine outcomes and goals
> ➢ Assign accountability
> ➢ Evaluate progress and re-align

● **Why is planning sometimes ignored or shortened? How do we know when our planning is complete?**

> *Plan your work and work your plan.*
> —Napoleon Hill

SOUND STRATEGY > EFFECTIVE MANAGEMENT > LEADERSHIP EXCELLENCE

Create Goals

Strategic objectives are almost always dependent on the successfully finishing intermediate goals or daily tasks. When we can break down our BHAG into its component pieces, we are able to realistically achieve extraordinary accomplishments.

SMART Goals

Since our most significant goal is our overall mission, all of our subordinate objectives should support its eventual achievement. These goals should possess the five characteristics listed below:

- Specific
- Measureable
- Achievable
- Relevant
- Time-explicit

> Which aspect of SMART goals if the most elusive to achieve? Which is the most critical? How will such goals enable our vision?

REFINED

Commitment: Refined Management

The quest for positive, exciting behavior change requires effort and stamina. It is for the strong-willed. In our workshop laboratory, we have explored activities contributing toward improved leadership. Continued practice and coaching will lead to mastery of the concepts and methods, ensuring solid, long-term results. Thank you for the authentic effort!

Prepare, Practice, and Report

Please prepare a Refined Management activity to practice outside of training and then report back to the lab participants. Consider your own development or the benefit of a co-worker when deciding who to involve.

I	Prepare details for your Refined Management commitment.

Refined Management Task:

Who to Involve:

Why This Is Important:

What I Will Do:

How I Will Do It:

  **REFINED**

Commitment Report Observations

As participants relate their commitment experiences, carefully watch their delivery. Note how they applied the principles we have discussed. Did they cover all aspects of the commitment? What specifically did they do well? Where were opportunities to coach for even more progress? What did you observe that you would like to appreciate, recognize, or adopt for yourself?

Observation Notes: Name, Compliment, Proof
1.
2.
3.
4.

Commitment Report Personal Debrief

Review the commitment report you just delivered. Consider your own input and feedback from the coach and fellow participants. List everything you did well, circling the one success that was most meaningful to you. Identify one challenge that will add the most leadership value to when improved.

All My Successes

_____

_____

_____

My One Greatest Challenge

_____

REFINED

Realized Benefits

We train to realize our vision, to develop tools to reach our goals, to become more excellent, and to assist others in doing the same. Having performed the related objectives, consider how they have moved us closer to attaining our vision and mission.

- [✓] Excellent
- [ ] Very good
- [ ] Good
- [ ] Average
- [ ] Poor

My Most Significant Benefit

Of all the benefits you may have experienced in this workshop, which one is the most significant for you, either professionally or personally? Why is this benefit essential to your leadership success?

_____

_____

_____

Benefitting Others

Our development serves to help those around us, our partners, teams, departments, and organizations. How will my most significant benefit impact those around me? Who in my circles of influence might also take advantage of this training to realize increased leadership success?

_____

_____

_____

_____

Transformation Project

As wise leaders know, training is an investment that can offer many kinds of returns, such as minimized employee turnover, increased sales, reduced expenses, amplified productivity, and greater customer satisfaction. Leadership training can provide some of the largest of returns on investment, especially to bottom line profitability. A Transformation Project is one way to demonstrate that ROI in hard numbers. Please speak with the coach about how this would be of use to your organization.

REFINED

Refined Summary

On our journey towards increased mission planning and management effectiveness, we have considered several concepts relating to becoming more refined. We discussed three objectives:

1. Align mission statements for future success
2. Welcome input to discover opportunities
3. Create goals to achieve better gains

There are a number of questions to contemplate as we summarize this workshop. What concepts will result in the most positive impact if applied regularly? Which ones should you put into action right away? Why are those key? Which principles will make the most difference for improved leadership in your work situation? How can I most benefit the team that I am responsible for leading? In which area do I need to improve the most?

■ **When implementing team missions and goals, what resistance will you expect from your supervisor? Subordinates?**

■ **How can we invite a hesitant team member to contribute to our green-light sessions? What will be the long-term effects?**

SOUND STRATEGY > EFFECTIVE MANAGEMENT > LEADERSHIP EXCELLENCE

REFINED

Refined Conclusion

In preparing for battle I have always found that plans are useless, but planning is indispensable.

—Dwight D. Eisenhower

Additional Notes

VIGOROUS MANAGEMENT
Doggedly Pursuing Quality

The summer soldier and sunshine patriot …

VIGOROUS

Becoming Vigorous

How are we to pursue our objectives? With fervor, determination, and zeal. If we are to perform an undertaking, why not put our best effort into it and do it right? Let us deliver an effort of exceptional quality, the fourth key characteristic of leadership. Whenever there is a job to be done, we should spurn the mediocre and embrace the superior.

Personal Insight: Vigorous

What does being vigorous mean to you? How does it relate to your current condition? In what ways will becoming more vigorous improve your situation?

_____

_____

_____

Quality and Vigorous

The power to perform at our best is liberating, but it needs to be tempered with discernment to know how to proceed in the optimal manner. Once those two conditions are met, we can attain great quality activities by throwing all of our might into the endeavor.

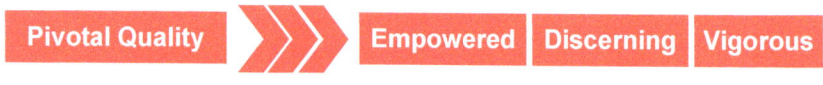

Management and Vigorous

Our team members are inspired when they see us as leaders pursuing our goals with energy and high levels of quality. We become respected as leaders because we are only interested in the finest of outcomes for ourselves, our team, and our customers.

VIGOROUS

Training Objectives

Workshop objectives represent small goals designed to help us develop the leadership characteristic being deliberated. They provide both clear direction for our training activities, and a method for measuring successful application of the related content. They connect to the leadership skills we evaluated as part of our self-assessment at the start of our training.

As we diligently embrace these objectives, we will perceive positive changes in our performance and personality.

Vigorous Training Objectives	♥
1. Accept the power of superior quality—excellence as an attitude—to maximize quality of outputs	
2. Foster innovation to attain robust breakthroughs	
3. Control processes and correct mistakes to reduce operational expenses	

Linking to Management

Think back to the vision and mission for increasing effective management that we considered at the beginning of the training. Reflect on how this characteristic relates to our desire to become more effective.

=	**How does becoming more vigorous support those aims? Why is increasing vigor critical to becoming a successful leader?**

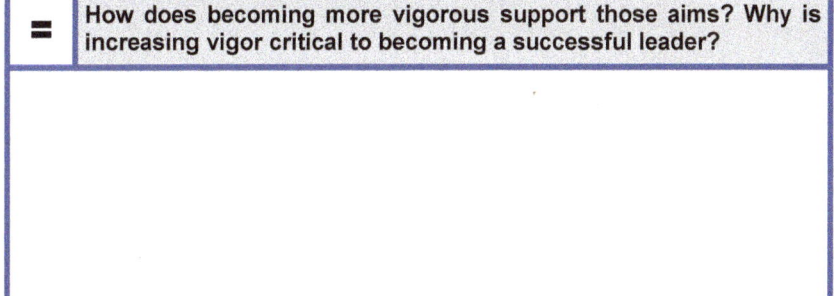

Always blaze the better path instead of grooming the popular route. Always pursue greatness over mastering mediocrity.
—David Benson

VIGOROUS

Power of Superior Quality

We live in a world of limited resources. There seems to never be enough investment capital, assets, or cash on hand for all of our projects. We always need more people, and yearn for more production and customers. We definitely do not have enough time, perhaps our most precious of all resources. How can we afford to devote any of it to developing our leadership capacity, or the skills of our teams?

The Unlimited Resource

While most resources are truly limited, excellent leadership has the potential for delivering truly unlimited outputs. Yes, engaged employees will work longer hours, but that cannot be sustained indefinitely. Fully engaged employees will also contribute their intellect, untapped talents, and problem-solving prowess. These donations can overcome many of the shortcomings of limited resources, and become an ocean of productivity for our organizations.

Excellence as an Attitude

Doing our best means different things in different situations. Sometimes, the path is very clear and direct, while at other times it is a bit more foggy and circuitous.

●	How does good leadership relate to an attitude of excellence?

Ways to Be Excellent

There are a number of clues by which we can we tell if our audience is receiving the same message we are sending, or if we have missed the mark with our efforts.

> ➢ Aim for the optimal, relevant outcome
> ➢ Give 100% effort
> ➢ Benefit from every failure
> ➢ Stay focused, optimistic, motivated
> ➢ Involve other people

VIGOROUS

Power of Superior Quality to Save Time

Let us do the math in a very limited way to demonstrate the power of high quality activities. Picture a typical business scenario comprising a substantial percentage of your profitability, a core activity for your company. Now contemplate all of the problems that might cause delays, missed project deadlines, or wasted time if the effort were left to disengaged employees.

> ➢ Planning errors
> ➢ Safety violations
> ➢ Production mistakes, rework
> ➢ Delays due to illness, low productivity, different priorities
> ➢ Reactivity instead of proactivity
> ➢ Miscommunication
> ➢ Arguments, hard feelings, anger
> ➢ Uncooperative, withholding resources
> ➢ _____ ?

Estimate the Damage

How much time would be lost if of the above problems occurred?

=	Calculate the potential lost time for a specific project at your office. Be realistic. Is it worth working towards high quality leadership?

Foster Innovation

We should always be seeking to progress. Incremental improvements are a part of staying competitive, keeping pace with our business rivals, and surviving. Innovation goes beyond continuous small advances to create huge leaps in performance, modernization, and profitability.

Innovation Process

When innovating, we face forward toward the future, expecting to shift paradigms, think outside of boxes, and invert best practices.

> **What is a key to innovation? How can we make innovating a regular part of our business?**

PIVOTAL QUALITY > EFFECTIVE MANAGEMENT > LEADERSHIP EXCELLENCE

Control Processes

When our work is out of control, it is difficult to ensure a desired level of quality. The work suffers because we are constantly focusing on matters that are not adding the most value.

Tyranny of the Urgent

Popularized by Stephen Covey, the original concept was by Charles E. Hummel in 1967.

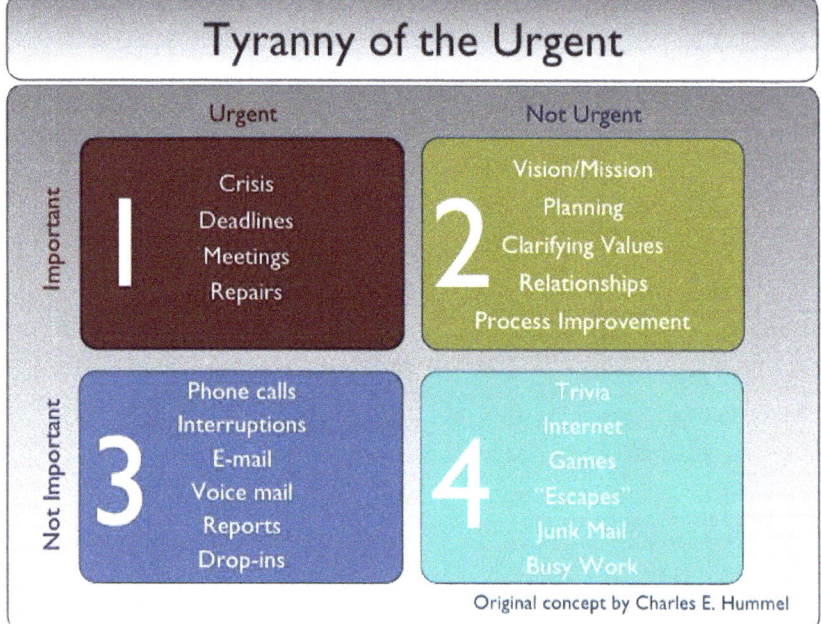

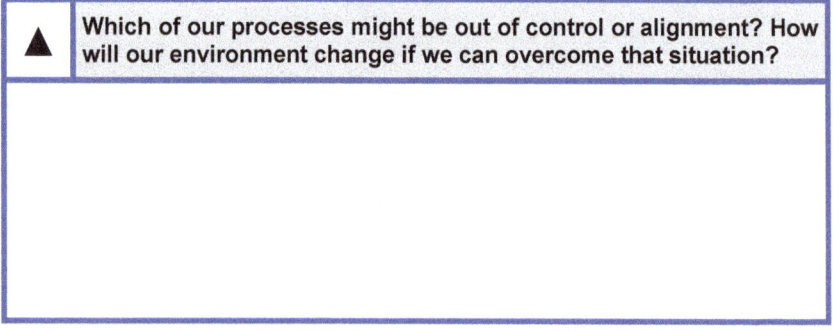

▲ **Which of our processes might be out of control or alignment? How will our environment change if we can overcome that situation?**

Correct Mistakes

In our pursuit of elevated quality, mistakes will happen and failures will result. This is inevitable, and if handled properly, can lead to accelerated successes and greater triumphs. By overcoming mistakes, we not only improve processes and discover innovative solutions, but we also increase the skills of our staff.

- Regularly review work
- Catch mistakes early and small
- Fix problem not people
- Capitalize on good relationship
- Encourage person
    - Common error, easy to overcome
    - Highlight talent, compliment
- Commit to solution

● **Practice overcoming a work-related mistake.**

A person who never made a mistake never tried anything new.
Albert Einstein

VIGOROUS

Commitment: Vigorous Management

The quest for positive, exciting behavior change requires effort and stamina. It is for the strong-willed. In our workshop laboratory, we have explored activities contributing toward improved leadership. Continued practice and coaching will lead to mastery of the concepts and methods, ensuring solid, long-term results. Thank you for the authentic effort!

Prepare, Practice, and Report

Please prepare a Vigorous Management activity to practice outside of training and then report back to the lab participants. Consider your own development or the benefit of a co-worker when deciding who to involve.

❗	**Prepare details for your Vigorous Management commitment.**

Vigorous Management Task:

Who to Involve:

Why This Is Important:

What I Will Do:

How I Will Do It:

PIVOTAL QUALITY > EFFECTIVE MANAGEMENT > LEADERSHIP EXCELLENCE

Commitment Report Observations

As participants relate their commitment experiences, carefully watch their delivery. Note how they applied the principles we have discussed. Did they cover all aspects of the commitment? What specifically did they do well? Where were opportunities to coach for even more progress? What did you observe that you would like to appreciate, recognize, or adopt for yourself?

Observation Notes: Name, Compliment, Proof
1.
2.
3.
4.

Commitment Report Personal Debrief

Review the commitment report you just delivered. Consider your own input and feedback from the coach and fellow participants. List everything you did well, circling the one success that was most meaningful to you. Identify one challenge that will add the most leadership value to when improved.

All My Successes

_____

_____

_____

My One Greatest Challenge

_____

VIGOROUS

Realized Benefits

We train to realize our vision, to develop tools to reach our goals, to become more excellent, and to assist others in doing the same. Having performed the related objectives, consider how they have moved us closer to attaining our vision and mission.

- ✓ Excellent
- ☐ Very good
- ☐ Good
- ☐ Average
- ☐ Poor

My Most Significant Benefit

Of all the benefits you may have experienced in this workshop, which one is the most significant for you, either professionally or personally? Why is this benefit essential to your leadership success?

_____

_____

_____

Benefitting Others

Our development serves to help those around us, our partners, teams, departments, and organizations. How will my most significant benefit impact those around me? Who in my circles of influence might also take advantage of this training to realize increased leadership success?

_____

_____

_____

_____

Impactful Facilitating

Already have a topic to present to your team and need someone to really make it engaging? Or just need an outside voice to lend credibility, add expertise, or support your own busy staff? We can add value and impact to your employee orientation, brain storming session, conflict resolution, problems solving exercise, or process improvement effort. Let our facilitation experience guide your teams to solid outcomes. Please speak with the coach if facilitating your next organizational event might be useful.

  VIGOROUS

Vigorous Summary

On our journey towards increased quality and management effectiveness, we have considered several concepts relating to becoming more vigorous. We discussed three objectives:

1. Accept excellence to maximize quality
2. Foster innovation for breakthroughs
3. Control and correct to reduce expenses

There are a number of questions to contemplate as we summarize this workshop. What concepts will result in the most positive impact if applied regularly? Which ones should you put into action right away? Why are those key? Which principles will make the most difference for improved leadership in your work situation? How can I most benefit the team that I am responsible for leading? In which area do I need to improve the most?

■ **Which of the concepts above will add the most value to your workplace if implemented? Why?**

■ **How can we use principles already discussed in the lab to overcome bad attitudes towards change, fires, and errors?**

PIVOTAL QUALITY > EFFECTIVE MANAGEMENT > LEADERSHIP EXCELLENCE

VIGOROUS

Vigorous Conclusion

Innovation distinguishes between a leader and a follower.

—Steve Jobs

Additional Notes

_____

_____

_____

_____

_____

_____

_____

_____

_____

_____

_____

_____

_____

_____

_____

COOPERATIVE MANAGEMENT
Forming Supportive Bonds to Thrive

United we stand ...

COOPERATIVE

Becoming Cooperative

We are better equipped to achieve our goals as we involve others who have the same objective. Together, the mutual drive propels us forward. Leaders and those who follow them become equally yoked in their efforts.

Personal Insight: Cooperative

What does being cooperative mean to you? How does it relate to your current condition? In what ways will becoming more cooperative improve your situation?

_____

_____

_____

Altruism and Cooperative

Leaders realize that they are able to do much good on their own, but can only do the MOST good if they cooperate with – and receive cooperation from – others intent on excellence. Bands strong and true can be created when we are altruistic, the fifth key characteristic of leadership. We cooperate with others not to achieve our personal ends, but because we have shared objectives, and our desire is for everyone to succeed.

Management and Cooperative

Esteem as a leader grows as we demonstrate concern not only for superior performance, but for utilizing methods that lift and develop others. Cooperation is then a united effort, with different roles combining to accomplish the joint result. All ships are lifted in a tide of success.

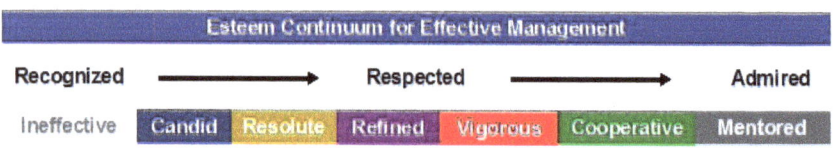

COOPERATIVE

Training Objectives

Workshop objectives represent small goals designed to help us develop the leadership characteristic being deliberated. They provide both clear direction for our training activities, and a method for measuring successful application of the related content. They connect to the leadership skills we evaluated as part of our self-assessment at the start of our training.

As we diligently embrace these objectives, we will perceive positive changes in our performance and personality.

	Cooperative Training Objectives	♥
1.	Actively listen to kindle respect and enthusiasm	
2.	Craft corrective discipline to maintain momentum	
3.	Master the meeting to augment reputation and productivity	

Linking to Management

Think back to the vision and mission for increasing effective management that we considered at the beginning of the training. Reflect on how this characteristic relates to our desire to become more effective.

=	How does becoming more cooperative support those aims? Why is increasing cooperation critical to becoming a successful leader?

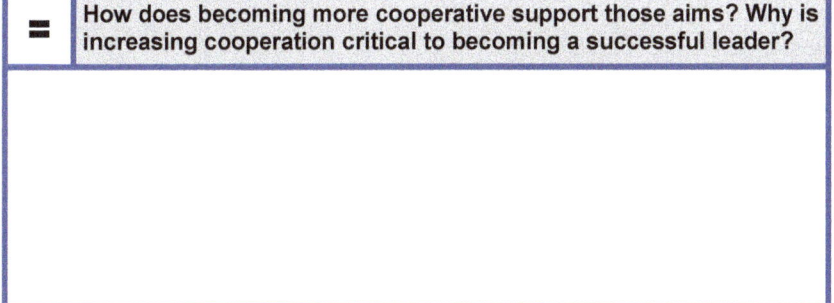

> *Competition has been shown to be useful up to a certain point and no further, but cooperation ... begins where competition leaves off.*
> —Franklin Roosevelt

Kindling Respect and Enthusiasm

Management by definition involved outside systems and people. Our employees make individual decisions to do their best, to put surplus, discretionary effort into the work they perform for their employers. Such exertion has the potential to benefit both parties, and in an ideal world it does. As our managerial esteem grows along the continuum, our employees increasingly wish to be fully involved with our team, but may still have some misgivings regarding the motivation of her employer.

The employer's customary loyalty is to shareholders (or the larger stakeholder concept), displayed by maximizing profits. Employees are means to that end, cogs in a wheel, and the steps of confidence, inspiration, embracing, and empowerment could all be seen as ancillary means to that same end. However, all doubt is cast aside as manager and employee cooperate, proving that they are both very much concerned for the welfare of the team and its members.

Actively Listen

We are not able to fully cooperate until we learn to listen actively and deliberately. Clear communication is a vital element of working together, and not something we can just hope will happen. When practiced appropriately, it also demonstrates that we are willing to treat our team members with respect, which increases their desires to contribute.

Listening Levels

Active listening requires that we practice open and friendly attitudes and body language. It also necessitates being fully present, and paying emotional and intellectual attention to the speaker.

- Ignoring
- Pretending
- Selective
- Attentive
- Empathetic

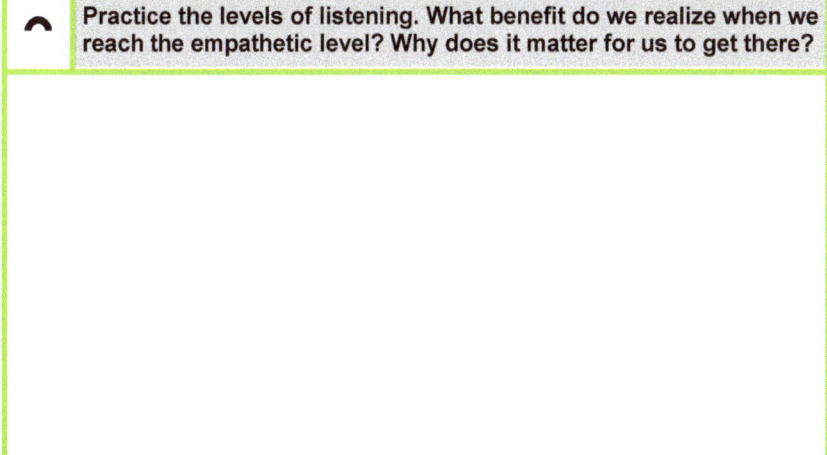

Practice the levels of listening. What benefit do we realize when we reach the empathetic level? Why does it matter for us to get there?

COOPERATIVE

Maintain Momentum

The structure of an organization demands that each person take on a formal role with attached responsibilities. The body performs best when it has its head, and hands, and legs intact. The team members recognizes this requirement as reasonable.

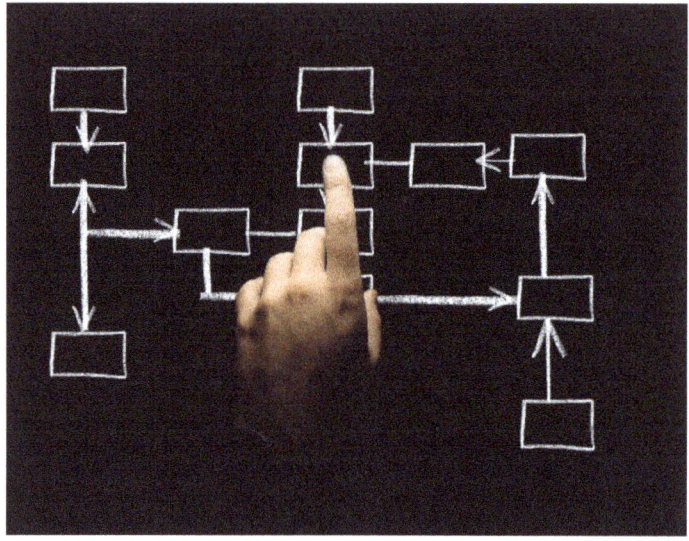

The organization recognizes that single elements work best when receiving support and direction from the whole. Yes, there is obviously room for individuality and personality, recognizing that there is more to its employees than the work they can perform. Still, the work must be of high quality and in an environment that respects order and results as well.

COOPERATIVE

Corrective Discipline

At times, our team members are not as enthusiastic about correcting mistakes as we would like. They may even deny that problems exists, or that their behavior is relevant, or they may resist solutions. It is in these delicate moments that our engagement and trust really pay off.

- Gather evidence beforehand
- Capitalize on good relationship
- State the concern fearlessly
- Relate to job description and buy-in
- Explain consequences
- Agree to solution: up or down

> How are disciplinary actions handled in your office? How might these steps encourage more cooperation?

> *Wisdom is the reward you get for a lifetime of listening when you'd have preferred to talk.*
> —Doug Larson

HEROIC ALTRUISM > EFFECTIVE MANAGEMENT > LEADERSHIP EXCELLENCE

COOPERATIVE

Augment Reputation and Productivity

As we work to improve our situation, our skills and influence grow. We become more pleased with our efforts, and desire to surround ourselves with people of the same mindset, those who may be very different from us in other respects, but share with us a desire to become the best that they can be. We also find that our reputation for getting things done, helping others, and making positive change becomes widespread.

Cooperation Spreads

Our progress influences other to cooperate with us. They start or continue to look for ways to be even better, basking in the shared reputation of competence and kindness. They help us find ways to lift our teams to higher heights.

> ● **What are some areas where our team members could become more productive? How have you tried to improve in this area?**

Master the Meeting

Meetings are one place where we can demonstrate our cooperative spirit. They are also where we can lose a lot of time and momentum. We schedule a meeting to get a status, and it ends up being an empty hour, or an opportunity to complain without finding solutions, or a chance to relax and avoid responsibilities. What are the criteria for your ideal meeting?

_____

_____

Meeting Structure

Always be ready to make the most of a meeting by preparing in advance and planning the event as you would a formal presentation or customer interaction.

- ➢ Clear purpose
- ➢ Location, start time, duration
- ➢ Agenda: written or verbal
- ➢ Determine participants
- ➢ _____
- ➢ Clear action items

> ▲ **What would you eliminate from current meeting practices? How would this change make a difference to your team?**

HEROIC ALTRUISM > EFFECTIVE MANAGEMENT > LEADERSHIP EXCELLENCE

COOPERATIVE   David Benson Coaching

Commitment: Cooperative Management

The quest for positive, exciting behavior change requires effort and stamina. It is for the strong-willed. In our workshop laboratory, we have explored activities contributing toward improved leadership. Continued practice and coaching will lead to mastery of the concepts and methods, ensuring solid, long-term results. Thank you for the authentic effort!

Prepare, Practice, and Report

Please prepare a Cooperative Management activity to practice outside of training and then report back to the lab participants. Consider your own development or the benefit of a co-worker when deciding who to involve.

I	**Prepare details for your Cooperative Management commitment.**

Cooperative Management Task:

Who to Involve:

Why This Is Important:

What I Will Do:

How I Will Do It:

Commitment Report Observations

As participants relate their commitment experiences, carefully watch their delivery. Note how they applied the principles we have discussed. Did they cover all aspects of the commitment? What specifically did they do well? Where were opportunities to coach for even more progress? What did you observe that you would like to appreciate, recognize, or adopt for yourself?

Observation Notes: Name, Compliment, Proof
1.
2.
3.
4.

Commitment Report Personal Debrief

Review the commitment report you just delivered. Consider your own input and feedback from the coach and fellow participants. List everything you did well, circling the one success that was most meaningful to you. Identify one challenge that will add the most leadership value to when improved.

All My Successes

_____

_____

_____

My One Greatest Challenge

_____

COOPERATIVE   David Benson Coaching

Realized Benefits

We train to realize our vision, to develop tools to reach our goals, to become more excellent, and to assist others in doing the same. Having performed the related objectives, consider how they have moved us closer to attaining our vision and mission.

- [✓] Excellent
- [ ] Very good
- [ ] Good
- [ ] Average
- [ ] Poor

My Most Significant Benefit

Of all the benefits you may have experienced in this workshop, which one is the most significant for you, either professionally or personally? Why is this benefit essential to your leadership success?

_____

_____

_____

Benefitting Others

Our development serves to help those around us, our partners, teams, departments, and organizations. How will my most significant benefit impact those around me? Who in my circles of influence might also take advantage of this training to realize increased leadership success?

_____

_____

_____

_____

Additional Training

We all know that excellence does not happen by accident. It takes dedication, persistence, and wisdom to make lasting, positive improvements to our leadership skillsets. This training event is one of many designed to develop our full potential as leaders. What other topics might benefit you or your organization? Please speak with the coach about recommendations for pursuing these very topics in more depth, or alternate topics that are critical to your ongoing success.

COOPERATIVE

Cooperative Summary

On our journey towards increased altruism and management effectiveness, we have considered several concepts relating to becoming more cooperative. We discussed three objectives:

1. Actively listen for respect and enthusiasm
2. Craft corrective discipline for momentum
3. Master the meeting for productivity

There are a number of questions to contemplate as we summarize this workshop. What concepts will result in the most positive impact if applied regularly? Which ones should you put into action right away? Why are those key? Which principles will make the most difference for improved leadership in your work situation? How can I most benefit the team that I am responsible for leading? In which area do I need to improve the most?

■ **Which of the above concepts will be the most difficult to implement? Why?**

■ **Which of the above concepts would you most like your supervisor to embrace? Why?**

COOPERATIVE

Cooperative Conclusion

> *The only thing that will redeem mankind is cooperation.*
>
> —Bertrand Russell

Additional Notes

_____

_____

_____

_____

_____

_____

_____

_____

_____

_____

_____

_____

_____

_____

_____

MENTORED MANAGEMENT
Advising as a Vital Investment

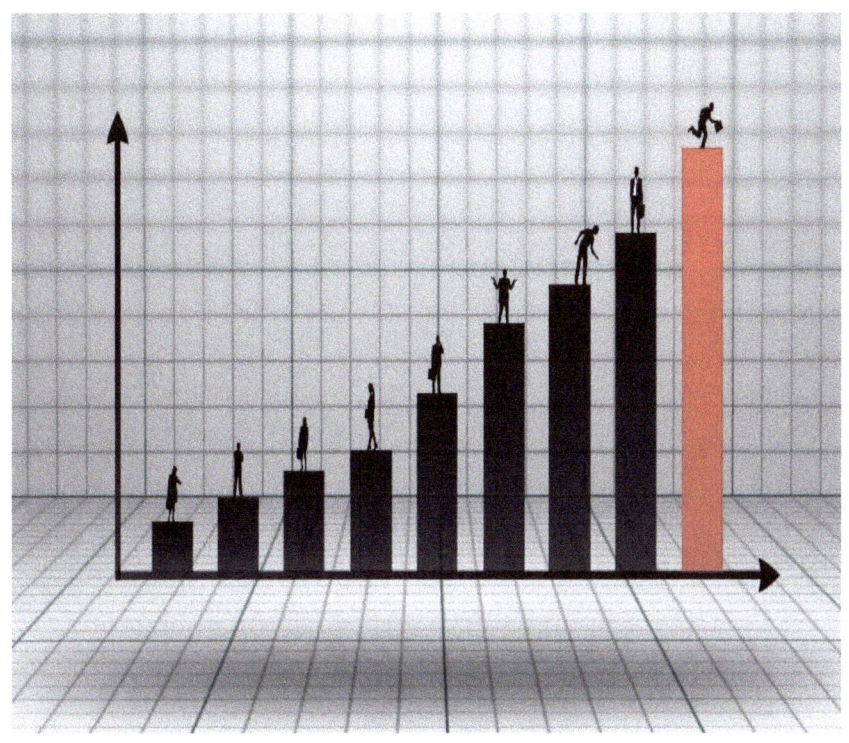

Put me in coach, I'm ready to play, today ...

MENTORED

Becoming Mentored

A mentor is an experienced, able, trusted counselor who is willing to invest effort and time and even reputation to support those she brings under her wing. Leaders mentor those for whom they are responsible to bring them to their own leadership level. Mentoring allows us to replicate our most valuable resource, more excellent leaders.

Personal Insight: Mentored

What does being mentored mean to you? How does it relate to your current condition? In what ways will becoming more mentored improve your situation?

_____

_____

_____

Coaching and Mentored

Mentoring represents the final phase of coaching, the sixth key characteristic of leadership. The coach is fully integrated in the success of her team member, devoting considerable energy to see her colleague and friend achieve greater heights.

Management and Mentored

As we work with our associates in a mentoring arrangement, they appreciate our work to help them succeed. Other members of our organization, and of our larger community, admire the relationship we possess, and recognize the victories that together we have acquired.

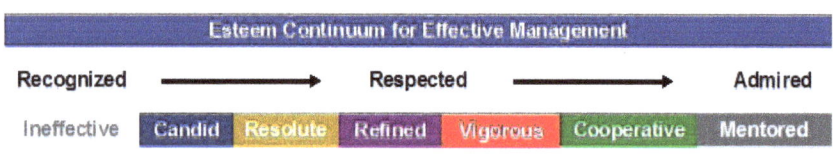

MENTORED

Training Objectives

Workshop objectives represent small goals designed to help us develop the leadership characteristic being deliberated. They provide both clear direction for our training activities, and a method for measuring successful application of the related content. They connect to the leadership skills we evaluated as part of our self-assessment at the start of our training.

As we diligently embrace these objectives, we will perceive positive changes in our performance and personality.

	Mentored Training Objectives	♥
1.	Regularly invest in personnel to sustain best practices	
2.	Stubbornly delegate to stretch successive leaders	
3.	Constructively mentor personnel to multiply quality	

Linking to Management

Think back to the vision and mission for increasing effective management that we considered at the beginning of the training. Reflect on how this characteristic relates to our desire to become more effective.

=	How does becoming more mentored support those aims? Why is increasing mentoring critical to becoming a successful leader?

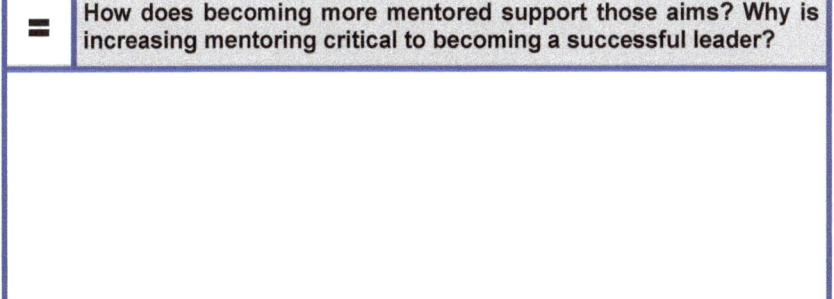

The delicate balance of mentoring someone is not creating them in your own image, but giving them the opportunity to create themselves.
—Stephen Spielberg

Regular Investment

Of all the resources available to us, none is perhaps as limited as our time. It is always shrinking, never growing, and thus very precious. We underscore the importance of our people as we spend more of our valuable time with them, supporting them, listening to them, mentoring them.

Who and How to Invest

Deciding who to mentor can be challenging, especially with many candidates and limited availability. How we mentor someone can take very different forms, though the act is significant enough to warrant a routine entry in our job descriptions, values and visions, and missions with subordinate goals.

> How do we decide who to mentor? In what ways do we invest in their progression? How can we make these activities regular?

Periodic Check-ups

Formal performance reviews should be a part of our regular staff investment, especially for those people we are mentoring. Just as previously discussed in the lab, these reviews ideally will engage our team members and encourage them to become increasingly accountable and proficient, while allowing the freedom to make their own decisions about where they are headed.

Train the Trainer

With mentees, this attitude becomes even more acute. In addition to the routine review, we take the approach that we are training the trainer, or preparing our replacement.

- Develop with an eye to leading
- More frequent evaluations
- Involve small groups
- Graduation?

> How does a mentoring check-up differ from a regular performance review? How would we check-up on multiple mentees a once?

Stubbornly Delegate

Once an interest grows beyond the ability of a single person to do it all, the growth of that interest could be considered nothing but delegation. Individual job responsibilities ultimately flow down from owners through management layers to the line operators. But delegation extends beyond that, crossing lines of role responsibilities to take on the assigned tasks.

Delegating = Deputizing

How to Delegate

Assigning tasks to another – dumping, dropping, distributing – by itself is not delegating. Authority to be successful must also be delegated.

> - Decide who
> - Create the plan
> - Implement the plan
> - Debrief

I — How does the effect of delegation change when the task is chosen before the person? Why is this still a valid approach?

When you delegate tasks, you create followers.
When you delegate authority, you create leaders.
—Craig Groeschel

Delegation Candidates

List co-workers, especially team members under your supervision, whom you would like see prepared for greater responsibility, a promotion, or who is being groomed for long-term succession. Which ones have the most potential, or are in need of the most mentoring, or could really make a difference in your larger organization? From our list of names, select one person to commit to mentoring within the next two weeks.

_____

_____

_____

Mentor the Mentor

Review the activities below that we have discussed to create effective management for ourselves and our teams. Which ones could be delegated as developmental projects? Circle one that would be the easiest to delegate right away for the above employee to start mentoring others.

Lead by Example	Excellence as an Attitude
Uncover Blind Spots	Foster Innovation
Establish Accountability	Control and Correct
Produce Internal Motivation	Actively Listen
Involve Customers	Craft Corrective Discipline
Vision Statement	Master the Meeting
Mission Statement	Periodic Check-ups
Welcome Input	Stubbornly Delegate
Create Goals	Constructively Mentor

MENTORED

Constructively Mentor

Probably the most important aspect of mentoring is to remain positive and optimistic. Focus on those behaviors and attitudes that support our goals, and flee from giving any more attention than needed to anything negative or pessimistic.

Replace to Overcome

Cognitive psychology suggests that we reward desired behavior to encourage it to grow, but that we ignore—not punish—undesired behavior to encourage it to shrink. The most profound way to eliminate *bad* behavior is to let it wither on the vine. Focus only on what we wish to endure.

> ■ **What obstacles will we face when attempting to be nothing but positive? How is it even possible?**

Resilient Attitude

Significant research has indicated that our attitude is paramount in determining the actions and behaviors we will exhibit. As we seek to mentor others and develop our own leadership capabilities, keeping a resilient attitude will allow us to keep the six leadership Characteristic top of mind, and allow us to progress.

- Prepare for challenges along the way:
    - External mocking, resistance
    - Internal mistakes, setbacks
- Temper expectations
- Smile in the face of adversity

 Practice a resilient attitude with your lab partners: you, support, and challenge. Who could be a real-life support to you?

MENTORED

Commitment: Mentored Management

The quest for positive, exciting behavior change requires effort and stamina. It is for the strong-willed. In our workshop laboratory, we have explored activities contributing toward improved leadership. Continued practice and coaching will lead to mastery of the concepts and methods, ensuring solid, long-term results. Thank you for the authentic effort!

Prepare, Practice, and Report

Please prepare a Mentored Management activity to practice outside of training and then report back to the lab participants. Consider your own development or the benefit of a co-worker when deciding who to involve.

I | **Prepare details for your Mentored Management commitment.**

Mentored Management Task:

Who to Involve:

Why This Is Important:

What I Will Do:

How I Will Do It:

21.10   CRUCIAL COACHING > EFFECTIVE MANAGEMENT > LEADERSHIP EXCELLENCE

Commitment Report Observations

As participants relate their commitment experiences, carefully watch their delivery. Note how they applied the principles we have discussed. Did they cover all aspects of the commitment? What specifically did they do well? Where were opportunities to coach for even more progress? What did you observe that you would like to appreciate, recognize, or adopt for yourself?

Observation Notes: Name, Compliment, Proof
1.
2.
3.
4.

Commitment Report Personal Debrief

Review the commitment report you just delivered. Consider your own input and feedback from the coach and fellow participants. List everything you did well, circling the one success that was most meaningful to you. Identify one challenge that will add the most leadership value to when improved.

All My Successes

_____

_____

_____

My One Greatest Challenge

_____

MENTORED

Realized Benefits

We train to realize our vision, to develop tools to reach our goals, to become more excellent, and to assist others in doing the same. Having performed the related objectives, consider how they have moved us closer to attaining our vision and mission.

☑ Excellent
☐ Very good
☐ Good
☐ Average
☐ Poor

My Most Significant Benefit

Of all the benefits you may have experienced in this workshop, which one is the most significant for you, either professionally or personally? Why is this benefit essential to your leadership success?

_____

_____

_____

Benefitting Others

Our development serves to help those around us, our partners, teams, departments, and organizations. How will my most significant benefit impact those around me? Who in my circles of influence might also take advantage of this training to realize increased leadership success?

_____

_____

_____

_____

Executive Coaching

Determined to supercharge culture and obliterate obstacles? Enlist our coaching services to make a lasting impact for your organization. Participants are held accountable for developing the improved skills and new habits they desire, with guided follow-up to ensure success. Executive coaching is also available for individuals ready to take their leadership game to the next level. Please speak with the coach if about executive coaching for your members of your organization.

MENTORED

Mentored Summary

On our journey towards increased coaching and management effectiveness, we have considered several concepts relating to becoming more mentored. We discussed three objectives:

1. Regularly invest to sustain best practices
2. Stubbornly delegate to stretch leaders
3. Constructively mentor to multiply quality

There are a number of questions to contemplate as we summarize this workshop. What concepts will result in the most positive impact if applied regularly? Which ones should you put into action right away? Why are those key? Which principles will make the most difference for improved leadership in your work situation? How can I most benefit the team that I am responsible for leading? In which area do I need to improve the most?

■ **Determine a topic for the other group to explore…**

■ **Determine a topic for the other group to explore…**

MENTORED

Mentored Conclusion

> *Every great achiever is inspired by a great mentor.*
> —Lailah Gifty Akita

Additional Notes

TRAINING CULMINATION
The Beginning of the Excellence

We'll remember always, Graduation day …

LEADERSHIP

Congratulations

Congratulations! Having attended all the training sessions and delivered on all the assignments, you have completed this training. Let us take a moment to look back on our experience together, and to celebrate our achievements.

Who Do You Appreciate?

Look around the room. Smile at your fellow participants. Review your notes in the workbook for insights they have related, or value they have added to the conversation. How have they modeled the principles and concepts we have discussed? What specifically have they done to inspire you? How have they clearly and unabashedly embraced the training? Why would you like to have each of them working on your team?

> ▲ Give and receive appreciation for contributing to our success in the Leadership Excellence Course. Be specific, and say thank you.

Complete Self-Assessments

Please finish the self-assessment table for each of the three leadership tracks we have studied together. Fill in the *after* column, calculate your personal improvement, and respond to the two open-ended questions at the bottom of each page. Finally, place a check mark in the boxes below for each track to signal that the self-assessments are complete.

Total Engagement	Dynamic Presentations	Effective Management

18 Workshops > 6 Series > 3 Tracks > Leadership Excellence Course

LEADERSHIP

Most Significant Benefit

Review the benefits you have listed for the past workshops. Of all the benefits you have experienced in this training, which one is the most significant for you, either professionally or personally? Why is this benefit essential to your leadership success? Who else will this impact?

Benefit _____

Why _____

Others _____

Complete Training Evaluation

Please finish the training evaluation on the next page for the entire training event. Then, place a check mark in the box to the right to signal that the evaluation is complete.

Now What?

With this training completed, there are a number of activities we can do to continue our quest for developing leadership excellence.

- ➢ Final assignment, email, online coaching
- ➢ Practice, teach, coach
- ➢ More training: self, others, new topics
- ➢ Speaking, facilitating, executive coaching
- ➢ Transformation project

> *There are a thousand hacking at the branches of evil to one who is striking at the root.*
> —Henry David Thoreau

LEADERSHIP

Training Evaluation

Please evaluate the completed training for each of the aspects below using a scale from 0-10 (*not at all* to *totally*). Enter column numbers rating your experience, and optionally provide your name at the bottom.

Training Aspects to Appraise (0 – 10)	Score
1. The concepts taught were sound and thorough.	
2. The concepts were clear and organized.	
3. Progression from one concept to another was smooth and logical.	
4. The coach's delivery was competent and effective.	
5. The coach was approachable and responsive.	
6. The coach helped me achieve my objectives.	
7. The participant materials were easy to use and follow.	
8. The participant materials enhanced the training for the better.	
9. I will apply the principles and techniques studied.	
10. I will recommend this training to colleagues and friends.	
Evaluation Totals (100 points max.)	

11. What was really great about this training? Why?

_____

_____

_____

12. What could have been better? Why? How?

_____

_____

_____

13. Additional training topics? _____

Name: _____ Organization: _____

LEADERSHIP

Transformation Project

As wise leaders know, training is an investment that can offer many kinds of returns, such as minimized employee turnover, increased sales, reduced expenses, amplified productivity, and greater customer satisfaction. Leadership training can provide some of the largest of returns on investment (ROI), especially to bottom line profitability. A Transformation Project can demonstrate the ROI of training in hard numbers, proving the impact of the concepts when they are implemented.

Transformation Project Proposal

Please follow this format when identifying the expectations and plans for the Transformation Project.

Integrity: describe the current situation in honest, candid terms. Relate the current problem or challenge, list who is involved, and provide concrete baseline data as a starting point for the project.

Motivation: identify a clear vision of what you want to replace the current situation. Explain why the change is important, what the ideal future state looks like, and what values are represented.

Strategy: create specific plans to achieve the vision. Provide a timeframe (no more than three months) with a mission statement, SMART goals, hard numbers, and unmistakable accountability.

Excellence, **Altruism**, **Coaching**: implement the plan. Explain how you will reach the projected goals. List the leadership characteristics and training insights or techniques that might be used. Track progress along the way, willing to adapt and reevaluate in order to succeed.

Report Project Results

At the conclusion of the Project, use the same format to compose a summary of the effort. Report on actual, measurable results over the duration of the project. Include both its impact on your organization's top and bottom lines (sales, profits, expenses, savings, etc.), and on your teamwork, culture, and attitudes. What is the anticipated annualized (or longer timeframe) effect? What will be the lasting influence of the Project, individuals, for your team, full organization, and larger community?

LEADERSHIP

Training Conclusion

Now this is not the end. It is not even the beginning of the end. But it is, perhaps, the end of the beginning.

—Winston Churchill

Additional Notes

_____

_____

_____

_____

_____

_____

_____

_____

_____

_____

_____

_____

_____

_____

_____

_____

References

All referenced materials are property of their respective copyright owners.

Avanogy.com. (2004). Retrieved https://www.learning-styles-online.com/overview/

Banaji, M. R., & Greenwald, A. G. (2016). *Blindspot: hidden biases of good people*. New York: Bantam books.

Benson, D. (2017). *Benson Scale: Standardized metrics for the hard and soft sciences*

Benson, D. (2017). *Leadership Excellence Model: The six core characteristics*

Blanchard, K., & Johnson, S. (2003). *The one minute manager*. London, United Kingdom: HarperCollins.

Brabandere, L. D., & Iny, A. (2013). *Thinking in new boxes a new paradigm for business creativity*. New York, NY: Random House.

Brown, B. (2015). *Daring greatly: how the courage to be vulnerable transforms the way we live, love, parent, and lead*. New York, NY: Avery.

Carnegie, D. (1995). *The leader in you: how to win friends, influence people and succeed in a changing world*. New York: Pocket Books.

Carnegie, D. (1998). *How to win friends & influence people*. New York: Simon and Schuster.

Carnegie, D. (2004). *How to stop worrying and start living: time-tested methods for conquering worry*. New-York: Pocket Books.

Chapman, G. D. (2010). *The 5 love languages, mens edition: the secret to love that lasts*. Chicago: Northfield Pub.

Cole, B., & Carnegie, D. (2012). *How to win friends and influence people in the digital age*. New York: Simon & Schuster Paperbacks.

Collins, J. (2001). *Good to Great*. Harper Business.

Collins, J. C., & Porras, J. I. (2009). *Built to last: successful habits of visionary companies*. New York, NY: Collins.

Connors, R., Smith, T., & Hickman, C. R. (2010). *The Oz principle: getting results through individual and organizational accountability*. New York: Portfolio.

Covey, S. M. (2014). *The speed of trust: the one thing that changes everything*. Simon & Schuster.

LEADERSHIP

Covey, S. R. (2007). *The 7 habits for managers managing yourself, leading others, unleashing potential*. New York, USA: Simon & Schuster.

Coyle, D. (2009). *The talent code: unlocking the secret of skill in sports, art, music, math, and just about anything*. Prince Frederick, MD: HighBridge Company.

Coyle, D. (2012). *The little book of talent: 52 tips for improving your skills*. New York: Bantam Books.

Csikszentmihalyi, M. (2008). *Finding flow: the psychology of engagement with everyday life*. New York, NY: Basic Books.

Dale Carnegie & Associates. (2012). *Emotional Drivers of Employee Engagement white paper*

Economy, P. (2015). *9 ways to make a great impression*. Retrieved from https://www.inc.com

Frankl, V. E. (2006). *Man's search for meaning*. Boston: Beacon Press.

Friedman, T. L. (2009). *The world is flat a brief history of the twenty-first century*. Brantford, Ont.: W. Ross MacDonald School Resource Services Library.

Gallup. *(2017). State of the American workplace report*

Gladwell, M. (2001). *The tipping point: how little things can make a big difference*. New York, USA: Back Bay Books.

Grant, A. M. (2014). *Give and take: why helping others drives our success*. New York: Penguin Books.

Grant, A. M. (2017). *Originals: how non-conformists move the world*. NY, NY: Penguin Books, an imprint of Penguin Random House LLC.

Grazer, B., & Fishman, C. (2016). *A curious mind: the secret to a bigger life*. New York: Simon & Schuster Paperbacks.

Koeppel, D. (2009). *Banana: the fate of the fruit that changed the world*. New York, NY: Plume.

Kondō, M., & Hirano, C. (2014). *The life-changing magic of tidying up: the Japanese art of decluttering and organizing*. Berkeley, CA: Ten Speed Press.

Lanigan, M. L. (2010). *How to create effective training manuals*. Retrieved from http://www.hpandt.com

Leadership and self-deception: getting out of the box. (2011). Richmond, British Columbia, Canada: ReadHowYouWant.

Lederman, M. T. (2012). *The 11 laws of likability: relationship networking-- because people do business* with people they like. New York: American Management Association.

Leeds, R. (2008). *One year to an organized life: From your closets to your finances, the week by week guide to getting completely organized for good.* Cambridge, MA: Da Capo/Life Long.

Lewis, C. S. (2017). *Surprised by joy: the shape of my early life.* San Francisco: HarperOne.

Markman, A. B. (2013). *Smart thinking: three essential keys to solve problems, innovate, and get things done.* New York, NY: Perigee/Penguin Group.

Marturano, J. (2014). *Finding the space to lead: a practical guide to mindful leadership.* New York: Bloomsbury Press.

Mattone, J. (2013). *Intelligent leadership: what you need to know to unlock your full potential.* New York: American Management Association.

Maxwell, J. C. (1993). *Developing the leader within you.* Nashville, TN: Thomas Nelson.

Maxwell, J. C. (2009). *How successful people think: change your thinking, change your life.* New York: Center Street.

Maxwell, J. C. (2012). *The 21 indispensable qualities of a leader: becoming the person others will want to follow.* Mumbai: Magna Publishing Co.

Miller, B. C. (2015). *Quick Team-Building Activities for Managers: 50 Exercises That Get Results in Just 15 Minutes* Ed. 2. Amacom.

Mind Tools Content Team. (n.d.). *Making a great first impression.* Retrieved from https://www.mindtools.com

Niemiec, R. (2016). *What are your "Defining Moments"?* Retrieved from http://www.viacharacter.org

Pink, D. H. (2012). *Drive: the surprising truth about what motivates us.* New York: Riverhead Books.

Robinson, K., & Aronica, L. (2009). *The element: how finding your passion changes everything.* New York: Penguin Books.

Rowh, M. (2012). *6 tips for making a good first impression.* Retrieved from http://www.apa.org

LEADERSHIP

Shipman, C., & Kay, K. (2014). *The confidence code: the science and art of self-assurance--what women should know*. New York, NY: Harper Business, an imprint HarperCollins.

Sincero, J. (2013). *You are a badass - how to stop doubting your greatness and start living an awesome life*. The Perseus Books Group.

Sinek, S. (2013). *Start with why: how great leaders inspire everyone to take action*. London: Portfolio/Penguin.

TINYpulse. (n.d.). Download: 2017 Employee Engagement Report. Retrieved from https://www.tinypulse.com/2017-employee-engagement-report-workplace-trends-culture-transparency-performance-reviews

The 30 Minute Expert Series. (2013). *Crucial Conversations…in 30 minutes*. Callisto Media, Inc.

Tracy, B. (2002). *Eat that frog!: 21 great ways to stop procrastinating and get more done in less time*. San Francisco, CA: Berrett-Koehler.

LEADERSHIP

About the Coach

David Benson, MBA
Leadership Coach

David Benson, Leadership Coach, is passionate about guiding business and community leaders to achieve their full potential. His business interests include leadership excellence, management integrity, motivating presentations, strategic planning, quality communication, unselfish employee engagement, and executive coaching. As a trainer and facilitator, he prefers an interactive approach to speaking that energizes audiences and challenges them to make immediate and significant improvements to their professional and personal lives.

David has over 25 years of experience in management consulting, corporate training, business analysis, and project management in a variety of fast-paced settings, from innovative start-up companies to industry powerhouses. The former Managing Director for Dale Carnegie Training of Utah, he was responsible for marketing, selling, and delivering content for professional development seminars and time-phased courses across the state. He has served as a consultant, presenter, and coach in the technology industry, advising over 100 small, large, and non-profit organizations at all supervisory levels.

David is the author of *The Poorest Man in Zion*, a series of cohesive essays on establishing a transcendent, thriving society rooted in principles of freedom, unity, virtue, diligence, charity, and continual improvement. A related but separate volume is planned for future publication under the title *A Practical Zion: The Companion Guide to The Poorest Man in Zion*, and expects to serve as a pragmatic blueprint for implementing the described behavioral principles in a contemporary setting.

Based on publications by the same name, David delivers ongoing *Leadership Excellence Seminar* and *Course* events across the United States. These in-person, full-day or time-phased training sessions focus on the six key characteristics of dynamic, engaging leaders that comprise his Leadership Excellence Model. A full-length, published examination of this model is forthcoming.

LEADERSHIP

In addition to dozens of technical certifications, David holds earned degrees in business (MBA, entrepreneurship specialization) from Utah State University, and in psychology (BS) from Brigham Young University. He is a veteran of the U.S. Army National Guard.

Raised in urban Virginia, he now resides in northern Utah with his wife and three of his six children. He enjoys kayaking, musical performance, and playing late-night family board games. His present, peculiar challenge is preparing for an Olympic-distance triathlon. Please visit www.DavidBenson.us for background and offering information.

Contact Details
David Benson Coaching
801-871-5804 office
435-760-0030 mobile
david@DavidBenson.us

www.ingramcontent.com/pod-product-compliance
Lightning Source LLC
Chambersburg PA
CBHW061215070526
44584CB00029B/3837